the
passionate
eye

the collected
writing
of suzanne vega

the
passionate
eye

SPIKE

AN AVON BOOK

AVON BOOKS, INC.
1350 Avenue of the Americas
New York, New York 10019

Copyright © 1999 by Suzanne Vega
Typography by Rhea Braunstein/RB Design
ISBN: 0-380-97353-7

Library of Congress Cataloging in Publication Data:
Vega, Suzanne.
   The passionate eye : the collected writing of Suzanne Vega.—1st ed.
     p. cm.
   "An Avon book."
   I. Title.
   PS3572.E334 P37 1999   98–47029
   818'.5408—dc21   CIP

First Spike Printing: March 1999

SPIKE TRADEMARK REG. U.S. PAT. OFF. AND IN OTHER COUNTRIES, MARCA REGISTRADA, HECHO EN U.S.A.

Printed in the U.S.A.

FIRST EDITION

QPM 10 9 8 7 6 5 4 3 2 1

introduction

What is in this book? Lyrics, mostly. I am a songwriter, and so the songs form the spine of the book, with poems and fiction and essays around them, supporting them, as it were.

Sometimes people ask me, where do I get my inspiration from? Three things: what I know to be true; what I see, especially in the streets of New York City; and what I imagine.

There are some poems included here that I wrote when I was very young. I include them because I ended up writing about the same subjects years later. What do I mean? The poem "By Myself" at age 9 becomes "Solitude Standing" at age 27. Some things never change, especially not in this particular life.

This book is about solitude, childhood, urban life, inner fantasy worlds, romance, violence, the mysteries of gender and appearances and glamour, the difficulties of communicating, and about faith and hope. There are chunks of my journals here, some taken from the years I've spent on the road traveling.

So I hope the writing here illuminates the world of the lyrics. In my fantasies it's the kind of book you pick through at different times of the day. Maybe you keep it in your desk at work, and take it with you to the bathroom, or maybe you sleep with it under your pillow. It should be a book that you dog-ear, that you write "How true!" or "This sucks!" or "What?" in the margins. Maybe it's something you'll return to at different times of your life. Maybe it will make you laugh.

I'd like to thank Bruce Miyashita for the title, and for his wonderful mind. I'd like to thank my family for believing in my talent. Thanks to Lou Aronica, Madeline Morel, and Mark James for their encouragement. Thanks to the Undertow for existing.

Thank you for reading this.

Suzanne Vega—1998

the
passionate
eye

SOLITUDE STANDING

Solitude stands by the window
She turns her head as I walk in the room
I can see by her eyes she's been waiting
Standing in the slant of the late afternoon

And she turns to me with her hand extended
Her palm is split with a flower, with a flame

Solitude stands in the doorway
And I'm struck once again by her black silhouette
By her long cool stare and her silence
I suddenly remember each time we've met

And she turns to me with her hand extended
Her palm is split with a flower, with a flame

And she says "I've come to set a twisted thing straight"
And she says "I've come to lighten this dark heart"
And she takes my wrist, I feel her imprint of fear
And I say, "I've never thought of finding you here"

I turn to the crowd as they're watching
They're sitting all together in the dark, in the warm
I wanted to be in there among them
I see how their eyes are gathered into one

And then she turns to me with her hand extended
Her palm is split with a flower, with a flame

And she says "I've come to set a twisted thing straight"
And she says "I've come to lighten this dark heart"
And she takes my wrist, I feel her imprint of fear
And I say, "I've never thought of finding you here"

Solitude stands in the doorway
And I'm struck once again by her black silhouette
By her long cool stare and her silence
I suddenly remember each time we've met

And she turns to me with her hand extended
Her palm is split with a flower, with a flame

by myself

(Age 9)

I stand by myself
Not lonely at all.
I listen to the little birds
Beckon and call.

I stand by myself
By the pond, with the fish
And now I don't even
Have one little wish

Except to be by myself
Each and every day
And come down to the woods
Where the little deer play.

AS A CHILD

As a child
You have a doll
You see this doll
Sitting in her chair

You watch her face
Her knees apart
Her eyes of glass
In a secretive stare

She seems to
She seems to
She seems to
Have a life

Pick up a stick
Dig up a crack
Dirt in the street
Becomes a town

All of the people
Depend on you
Not to hurt them
Or bang the stick down

And they seem to
They seem to
They seem to
Have a life

As a child
You see yourself
And wonder why
You can't seem to move

Hand on the doorknob
Feel like a thing
One foot on the sidewalk
Too much to prove

And you learn to
You learn to
You learn to
Have a life

written after a triumphant fight

(Age 12)

I'm the baddest girl in the world
I'm as bad as Super Fly
and I don't need coke to get me high.
I can beat you, Jack
and you better get back
when the Vega's come around.
We'll kick your ass, and make it last,
I got evil eye, and you sure gotta try
to put me on the ground.
I don't play, hey, you know what I say
when I say it or pay.
I can stare you down,
make you crawl on the ground.
I'm action, no talk, when I say to you walk, I'm not the
kind you can knock.
I use only my hands, no bottles for me
But I got plans, and you won't go home free.
When I don't smile, you know you're in trouble
'cause I can get wild, I ain't got no double.
I can make you cry, I can make you wanna die.
No one beat me yet, and they ain't gonna get the
chance.
I can take mine and the little folks at the same time.
I'm the baddest girl in the world.

fighting with boys

Some girls are taught to be sexy. L.A. girls for example. There you are taught to be blond and cute and show a lot of skin. It's different in New York. There you have to prove yourself, and you can't let any other kids mess with you. Not girls, and not boys. Boys will say stuff to you to see if you can take it, talk about your shoes, pull your hair, call you names, like, Hey, white girl, are you really a girl or a faggot? So you have to fight. Here are the rules.

Go for the biggest one. That was my father's advice. If you have to fight a crowd of boys, it's best to go for the biggest one. That way you won't have to fight them all. The others will see that you mean business, and you will have won their respect.

Call their bluff. If Tony W. picks up a lead pipe and swings it at you in the school hallway, he is bluffing. There's no way he'll hit you with it. This later was proven wrong, when Tony W. in fact did hit me in the ribs with a wooden board, as I went after him in the street. I chased him for blocks and returned to see the younger grades of the school out on the stoop cheering.

Defend what's yours. If my brother has provoked a fight by calling Tony W. a fucking bastard, then I still have to jump in and defend my brother. If everyone is standing around in a circle downstairs chanting, "The Vegas are sick, they suck on big dick," then you must go, and fight all of them, and make them stop, even if you are happily reading Steinbeck's *Travels with Charley* and do not want to go. You have to defend your honor. And your family.

Always aim for the face and the stomach. And always defend your own face and stomach. I forgot to do this once in the fight with Jonathan R. He hit me in the stomach, and knocked the wind out of me, after which my face hit the sidewalk and I chipped my front tooth.

Fight fair. But don't be stupid. It's best to fight fists with fists. That's the best, most honorable way. If you really need help, you can pick up a bottle and smash it against the curb and brandish the jagged edges at your opponent. Or else look for a stick, a lead pipe, a piece of wood. Switchblades are showy, as in *West Side Story*, but we never used them. Chains are for the more advanced, and guns are right out. You are trying to fight the guy, not kill him. This was twenty years ago, so I'm sure some of the rules have changed by now.

Never back down. Don't threaten something and then not do it, (See Call Their Bluff, above.) I came close to backing down once, when I offered to fight Ricky W. I remember saying, "Do you want to fight?" The words popped brightly out of my mouth before I had a chance to bite down hard on them, and I remember Ricky W.'s look of amused amazement, since he was the blackest, toughest, meanest guy in the school. Although he was thirteen, there were rumors that he had a woman in her early twenties, that he'd gotten her pregnant.

So when he turned his cold eyes in my direction and said, "Fight? Yeah, I'll fight you. I haven't had a fight in a while. I could use the exercise," and he began to roll his sleeves up over his hard tan muscles, I thought I was going to die. The other kids on the stoop said, "No, Suzy. Don't, Suzy," and looked at me nervously. I don't think I actually said anything or did anything after that except stare at him, and eventually the whole thing blew over, as he didn't take it seriously. I was relieved, but at least I had saved face.

Don't fight with girls. Girls are crazy and mean. They don't fight fair. Fighting fair means hard tight fists and regular punches. But girls will slap, bite, pinch, pull your hair, rip the buttons off your shirt and the earrings out of your ears.

The one exception was the fight with Carla W., where she had challenged me. We never even touched each other. I just stood there staring at her as she wound herself down, and she eventually began speaking nonsense. "I'll kick you in the ass! I'll kick you in the pussy and two babies will fall out!" What was that supposed to mean? Eventually the crowd around us began to laugh, and I was the winner.

The other fight with a girl was in high school. We were both fifteen. That was the last fight I ever had. She was a cute blond girl who besides being a ballet dancer, also worked as a model. We did not like each other. She accused me of having the Evil Eye, after which I called her mother a whore. She flew at me with her friend and pulled my braids. There are no rules in fights with girls. Just hurting.

I remember two girls fighting in my elementary school. They were wild: sobbing, crying, slapping, and punching each other, two light-skinned black girls, or maybe one was Puerto Rican. One had torn the other one's dress wide open and you could see her small hard breasts under her undershirt, exposed to the breeze, and the buttons from her dress rolling away down the asphalt. We all hung around, watching.

Sometimes you become friends afterward. This happened with Stephan D., a big, half-black, half-Jewish guy who hit me in the eye, after I hit him for some reason, which is unknown to me now. He hit me really fast. My eye swelled up. The crowd separated us before either of us could get in another hit. The teacher made us stay in after school to talk things over, and we actually became friendly. I still have the plastic bracelet he gave me at the end of the school year, striped with one stripe brown, one stripe red.

Even pacifists fight. "One of these days you Vegas will learn that violence is not the answer!" shouted my teacher Ruth M., as I held Michael E.'s face against the floor in the hallway. I had him down but never knew quite what to do after that, as I had no natural killer instinct. She forced me to let him up, and soon after that year, she quit teaching to enter New York politics. She is currently Manhattan Borough President, and is probably fighting some boys herself.

fight

(Age 12)

Apple Jacks and Vaughn
Are having a fight.
Vaughn is having fun
But Apples is uptight.

Apple Jacks and Vaughn
Are rolling on the floor.
Sophie comes and asks,
"Hey, what's the score?"

Rodney comes and answers,
"It's as plain as can be
Vaughn is gonna win
You just wait and see!"

Apple Jacks and Vaughn
Are having it out.
Vaughn is going easy,
And Apples wants to shout.

Ruth comes along
To break up the fight,
Sophie says to Rodney,
"How do you know you were right?"

Apple Jacks and Vaughn
Were having a fight.
Vaughn was having fun
But Apples was uptight.

my friend MILLIE

I was six years old and playing in the front yard on East 109th Street, with a stick and a crack in the sidewalk, when this big girl came up to me and said,

"Millie told me

that you

called me a huah

and I'm gonna knock your

fucking teeth down your throat."

I looked up and said, "Excuse me?" because I wasn't sure if I had heard her correctly.

She repeated her words.

Oh, I said, and tried to imagine what she was talking about. What was that word? A huah? What was that? I tried to picture this word in my head. I had just learned to spell the words "cough" and "bough." Perhaps this mystery word had a *gh* or a silent *p* in it. So I said,

"How do you spell that?"

My question took her by surprise; I could see it in her eyes, as she looked down at me. She thought for a second, then leaned forward, and said gently and dangerously into my face,

"I don't know how you fucking spell it. But it means a bad girl and if you call me it again I'll kick your fucking ass."

Then, looking over the small crowd that had gathered, she sought out the one face that wouldn't meet her eye and said,

"Millie. This girl ain't call me a huah. She don't even know what it is."

"Oh, yes, she did!" said my friend Millie. This did not surprise me as Millie would say anything. Millie would say, "Go inside and tell your mother it's my birthday." Which I would dutifully do. "Millie has her birthday five times a year," said my mother. "Go outside." I puzzled over that one. Millie has five birthdays? But now Millie stood there in front of the big girl, and in front of Markie, and the two little twins, and everyone else, and said "Yes, yes, she did, I swear to God she did."

But the crowd began to look at her suspiciously. Then they started in on her.

"How come you can't just swear? How come you gotta swear to God?"

And I breathed a sigh of relief, since I knew I was out of the hot water and she was falling in.

But Millie was just that way. My parents had taught me, do not talk to strangers. Do not accept gifts of any kind. Do not accept food as it will be poisoned, or it will have a hidden razor blade inside which will slice me up.

So one day I was in the front yard again, playing with a mysterious round object with a small window through which something blue was gleaming; now I would call it a blown fuse. I shifted it this way and that and poked at the glass. This was interrupted by a fat lady walking past the yard. She looked at me, and I looked at her, and then she did the unthinkable—she offered me candy.

"Would you like one?"
"No, no," I said.
"They are very good. Here have one," she said.
"No, I can't," I said, in a quiet panic.
"I'll leave it right here," she said, putting it onto the metal fence, in between the spikes. "In case you change your mind."

She sailed up the street. I went over to look at what I couldn't have. I didn't touch it. It was a piece of jelly candy, shaped like a section of orange, covered in sugar, and smiling in the sun at me.

I looked at it. I swear it looked back at me. I could feel it sort of singing to me. But I didn't touch it. So here comes my friend Millie walking down the street.

"Hey, what's this?" she says, snatching up the piece of candy. "Is this yours?"

"Some lady gave it to me. But don't eat it. It's got poison," I said, trying to be helpful.

She examined it. She popped it into her mouth.

I watched her, wondering if she would go blue in the face and drop dead, if blood would spurt from her mouth because of the razor blades, but she just chewed it, and swallowed it, and put her feet on the bottom of the gate.

"It's good," she informed me. "You are an idiot."

She swung around on the gate, and looked at me.

"Go ask your mother if I can have dinner here."

Last time I did that my mother had suggested that Millie eat at her own house.

"I don't know if I want to," I said.

"Go do it," she said, swinging on the gate, with her bony elbows sticking out. "Or I will go into the street and pull up my dress."

This puzzled me. Why would she do that? What did one have to do with the other?

"No, I don't think so," I said.

"Okay, then," she said, hopping off the gate.

She walked over to the curb, and lifted up her dress in a fast swooping motion in front of some kind of car going by. I wasn't sure why, but I felt worried, and thought maybe I should go in and ask my mother if she could stay for dinner, though I didn't want to.

"Maybe I will," I said nervously.

She ignored me and lifted up her dress again, and this time pulled down the front of her panties. A truck driver yelled something as he went around the corner in his truck. I was impressed.

"Okay," I said. Dinner with Millie meant hours of playing house where I was always the Baby, where whoever finished eating dinner last was a Rocking Egg, along with an endless commentary on what I had, what I wore, and what I did. But she was my friend, and she was bigger than me, so it was better than nothing.

Some time later we moved from that neighborhood to the Upper West Side. The day we left, we put our piano in the front yard to be moved. Some people came with a truck and loaded it up in front of all the neighbors. We never saw it again. Millie came to say goodbye.

"Maybe I could go with you," she said to me.
"No, I don't think so."

"I think my parents would let me go with you. It would be okay."
"No, that's okay," I said.

Many years later I was walking down the street, pondering the mystery of the word *huah* with the hidden *gh*—huaugh, maybe? and then it dawned on me what she had meant. She meant whore, like a prostitute. I had to laugh. Because if she had pronounced it the way they pronounced it in my first grade class, she would have said ho. You called me a *ho*. And I would have known what she meant because everybody knew what a ho was.

(Story told onstage)

NEIGHBORHOOD GIRLS

"We had our
Neighborhood girl, she
Used to hang out, in front of
McKinsey's Bar, and we
    were
Interested in her, and her
Clientele . . .
We just wonder where
    she's gone . . ."
"Oh she's gone?"
"Yes, she's gone, gone,
    gone."

"I think I know your
Neighborhood girl, she
Lives on my street, now,
    with
Eyes of ice
I've seen her in the morning,
    when she is
Walking in the sun
And I always thought that
    she
Looked kind of nice

She spoke to me once
At a party, I think
And I thought at the time
That she had had too much
    to drink, because she
Said to me, 'There's a
    backbone gone
And I've got to get it back
Before going on . . .'

And your neighborhood girl
Seems to have resigned
She was looking out at
    people
From the back of her mind

And before she went off
She spoke to me again
She came up and said,

'You have the eyes of a
    friend
And there's a razor's edge
That I have lost somewhere
And I would like it back
So if you've seen it any-
    where . . .
I've been out for a while
But I'll be back in a bit
I am just walking through
    the smoke
Finding out if this is it
Because I've got this feeling
That things are going gray
And I'd like to hear a
    straight line
To help me find my way . . .'

I looked at her
And I did not know what
    to say.
She had long black hair."
"Must be a different
Neighborhood girl, cause
Ours had blond hair, in
    front of
McKinsey's Bar
And we were interested in
    her
And her
Clientele
We just wonder where
    she's gone . . ."
"Oh she's gone?"
"Yes, she's gone, gone,
    gone."

for l.r.

You remind me of the day
when I first left home
you remind me of the moment
I learned I was really alone
you remind me of every boy
that I've ever known
from the first grade to the last ones

of the dust on the pavement
and the heat on the roof
of every closed fist
of every inner blade
you need to wake up with
you remind me of the edges
of the places in my life.

Believe me you don't
frighten me
you already know
the things I've seen

of the kids in the sprinklers
and dampness in the air
of every mother's hand
on every child's hair

You walk down
all of the streets in my life
and you know
every corner.

DANIELLA

(Age 16)

Daniella, she sits by the tree in the playground,
sometimes we go there and the children all play.
But no one can tell me just where is Daniella
when she looks in the distance that way.

Daniella, your hair is growing wild like a jungle,
like a garden of ivy that's been blown by the wind.
In the morning we brush it and tie it with a ribbon,
and in the evening it has flown loose again.

In the afternoon when the day seems forever
and the night feels like never then she will sigh.
But no one can tell me just where is Daniella
when her thoughts wander off to the sky.

Ilana's her friend, she runs fast like a squirrel,
she has big brown eyes and sometimes she cries.
But she stops very soon and they both play together,
making castles and strawberry pies.

And sometimes Daniella believes she's a sparrow,
she sits by the window and eats sunflower seeds.
She watches the rain and the birds on the rooftops,
and often I wonder just what she sees.

In the afternoon when the day seems forever
and the night feels like never, then she will sigh.
Oh no one can tell me just where is Daniella
when her thoughts wander off to the sky.

IRONBOUND/
FANCY POULTRY

In the Ironbound section near Avenue L,
where the Portuguese women come to see what you sell
the clouds so low, the morning so slow
as the wires cut through the sky

The beams and bridges cut the light on the ground
into little triangles and the rails run round
through the rust and the heat
the light and sweet coffee color of her skin

Bound up in iron and wire and fate
watching her walk him up to the gate
in front of the ironbound school yard

Kids will grow like weeds on a fence
She says they look for the light, they try to make sense
They come up through the cracks
Like grass on the tracks
She touches him good-bye

Steps off the curb and into the street
the blood and feathers near her feet
into the ironbound market . . .

In the Ironbound section near Avenue L,
where the Portuguese women come to see what you sell
the clouds so low, the morning so slow
as the wires cut through the sky

She stops at the stall
fingers the ring
opens her purse
feels a longing
away from the Ironbound border

"Fancy poultry parts sold here,
Breasts and thighs and hearts,
Backs are cheap and wings are nearly free,
Nearly free . . ."

blue sky and blood on tenth avenue

(The *New York Times Magazine*, November 20, 1988)

When I was growing up I spent five years in Spanish Harlem and ten years on the Upper West Side. The streets were always crowded with different types of people: kids from the projects, white liberals, students from Columbia. But I didn't hang out much. You could find me in my room, or in the park by the river. Facing south on an afternoon and seeing the angles of sunlight gave me a weird sense of orientation. As a child, I felt: "The sun is there. It's high and on my right. I am here. Everything is OK." As an adult I had stopped going to the park on the weekends, and that feeling rarely, if ever, visited again.

So it was about four o'clock on a cold Sunday, and I was out walking downtown. At Tenth Avenue and Fourteenth Street, or thereabouts, suddenly the rest of the city fell away, and I felt that same weird sense of orientation. I was in the meat market area.

The buildings in front of me were long and low, and the sky seemed very wide and intensely blue. It was a shock after the relentless verticality of the city behind me. Because of the cobblestone streets, the tin doors with porthole windows like a ship's kitchen, the ivy on the bricks, the river on my right, I thought for a minute I was somewhere else. Cannery Row, maybe.

It was quiet and still, with a lonely feeling. A strange landscape of cool, fat shadows and slices of dazzling sun on tin. Later, when I lived on Horatio Street, where the meat market ends, I learned the neighborhood's other moods and faces, but four o'clock on a Sunday afternoon is still my favorite time of day there.

If you look past the serene surface, you find clues to the violence beneath. The most obvious are the painted signs, worn and flaking: "Baby

Lamb! Young Kid! Fancy Poultry!" "Breasts, Thighs, Hearts, Livers, Wings." "Boxed Beef." Words that in another context can be sensual, or tender, or playfully erotic, here read like pornography or skewered poetry.

The elevated tracks with their big metal beams seem to shelter this empty place. Pigeons roost under these beams, and fly freely where their relatives are slaughtered every day. Little rivers of blood run along the cracks in the sidewalk, mixing with the sawdust. Or your foot is surprised by a skid of animal fat, white and greasy.

It feels like an underworld. If you see anyone, it might be a man with a wool cap and a big belly and a cigar. He doesn't want you looking at him or minding his business. There is an atmosphere of unseen deals, people watching and being watched, violence about to happen.

And at night when the meat shops close, the other "meat shops" open—the transvestites begin peddling after dark. What are they selling, exactly? I'm not sure. Things are displayed, discussed, bargained for and maybe sold in a quick sleight-of-hand; you see it only from the corner of your eye, as you walk by fast or speed past in a car. Long, thin mincing men, swaybacked and fiercely feminine, parade on the corners, their skinny masculine legs tottering in high heels and ragged pantyhose. Sometimes there is a bonfire, and you see a few of them, with one womanly man dressed in what seems to be a bathing suit and a full-length fur coat, calling to you, laughing, preening, fixing his lipstick. The graffiti reads: "Silence = Death." "Linda, I love you. Frank."

In the morning, though, the place bustles. That's the time I'm least familiar with. It's crowded with trucks and truckers—to get anywhere you wind and dodge your way through a thick traffic of men in bloody white aprons and slabs of meat swinging on hooks. By two in the afternoon it has settled down. By four o'clock it has regained the stoic feeling of an Edward Hopper painting, with calm cubes of color and long rectangular shadows, and a soft windy rustle of pigeons and the river.

underworld man

Don't stand in the scan
Of the underworld man.
Don't return his look.
Your eyes give so much
Information
That you will surely
Give yourself away again.

This is
The business.

Keep yourself
To yourself.
You don't ask,
You don't question,
You don't stop to ask direction.

graffiti

Peligro.
No pase.
Judy loves John.
Watch the cars
along the piers
Cruise until dawn.

tokyo

Crowded city
Each person carries
a solitude with them.
Keep your privacy
in your pocket.
So you may have it
as you wish.

osaka

*I am feeling rather evil
and feeling kind of mean.
I think I'll go to Mickey's
and check out the scene.*

*Three young boys are in there
downing the caffeine.
Either priests or gangsters
or something in between.*

Mickey's Café is a café in Osaka under the train tracks, under the elevated subway. So every five minutes the walls rumble, the coffee cups rattle, the comic books shake, everything flies up in the air and then it all settles.

Three boys sit at a table. Their heads are shaved. They could be priests, they could be a gang. Two wear black-rimmed glasses. All of them smoke. Watching one get up to use the toilet I decide they must be a gang. Although they could be priests.

A woman who could be their grandmother sits with them—she's hungry and eats for two hours straight. She stays after they go. Eats noodles in broth.

You are drunk and playing video games. You pass me a pornographic comic book. I laugh. You make me laugh.

A beautiful woman who looks like a secretary sits demurely in the corner, until she plays video games. Then she is in spasms, her lovely body crashing against the machine, her face frowning in concentration as she jerks the knobs.

betty the waitress

Why are you so nervous
and timid and shy?
Betty the waitress at Tom's
screams at me one night,
when we've gone for coffee.
Speak up!

She's near ninety I think
with curled hair and high heels
and red lipstick and her
tray balanced on her arm
and her lips in a sneer.

Hello, Bebe, she says when
she's feeling calmer, and
drags on a cigarette.

I am sitting
In the morning
At the diner
On the corner

I am waiting
At the counter
For the man
To pour the coffee

And he fills it
Only halfway
And before
I even argue

He is looking
Out the window
At somebody
Coming in

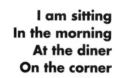

TOM'S

"It is always
Nice to see you"
Says the man
Behind the counter

To the woman
Who has come in
She is shaking
Her umbrella

And I look
The other way
As they are kissing
Their hellos

I'm pretending
Not to see them
Instead
I pour the milk

I open
Up the paper
There's a story
Of an actor

Who had died
While he was drinking
It was no one
I had heard of

And I'm turning
To the horoscope
And looking
For the funnies

When I'm feeling
Someone watching me
And so
I raise my head

There's a woman
On the outside
Looking inside
Does she see me?

No, she does not
Really see me
'Cause she sees
Her own reflection

And I'm trying
Not to notice
That she's hitching
Up her skirt

And while she's
Straightening her stockings
Her hair
Has gotten wet

Oh, this rain
It will continue
Through the morning
As I'm listening

To the bells
Of the cathedral
I am thinking
Of your voice . . .

And of the midnight picnic
Once upon a time
Before the rain began . . .

I finish up my coffee
It's time to catch the train

DINER

manhattan

(Age 15)

No sun
         could ever heal
this bruised piece of land
No sun
         could ever
                  send these buildings
                           skipping down the street
         there it is now
rising
         a streaking flash
against a cold city
. . . the buildings merely reflect
the sun's myriad colors
                  and do not grow with its warmth
poor things

THE BOULEVARDIERS

I like you
and you like him
and he likes me
and we all love each other.
We like to sit in the café
and eat and drink and talk
    all day
and watch the sun.
We like to read the news-
    paper
and talk about him and her
and who is getting along
    with who these days,
and when the sun goes
    down
we walk along the cobble-
    stone ground.

He loves the city
with the bricks and broken
    bottles
and the pretty little flowers
as they grow against the
    wall.
He is dark,
he is tall,
he is the tallest one of all
of us.
You are bright and quick
    and fair
and seems that you have
    lost some hair
but this is all right.
This is OK. We do not mind.
We write and fight and sing
and this is fine.

We drink the wine
if we get it free
and if he buys you coffee
he can surely buy some for
    me

and one day we will work
    real hard
and get a job
and not just sit here
writing letters
on this silly boulevard.
And everyone will know
    our name
and we'll be rich
or we'll at least
have some kind of fame.
We'll be brave,
we'll be bold,
we'll come riding through
like knights of old.

The sun is like
a lover's hand
as it comes down
and touches you
touches me
touches him
touches you.
And we have all got dirty
    feet
from wearing sandals in
    the street,
and we should all go home.
But still you will
insist insist
until each last one has
    been kissed
and each one is happy.
And when the sun goes
    down
we walk along the cobble-
    stone ground.
This is OK. We do not mind.
We write and fight and sing
and this is fine.

I am sitting by my window;
I am thinking of my rent.
I am looking through my pockets,
and I'm wondering where it went.
I am feeling like the Devil,
maybe like the Devil's wife.
I am singing for my supper.
I am singing for my life.

Things go up and things go down,
and we have all these highs and lows,
are we even in the end?
I don't think anybody knows,
but when I look from my window
I pretend that I'm in France.
You know I never have been there
but I might jump at the chance.

Tell me what do you do
with a troubled mind?
Do you sing? Do you cry?
Do you wait for a better time?
Do you think about tomorrow
when you're living in today?
And can you stop this tide against you,
make it go the other way?

And when I look from my window
I can hear the little bird sing;
And I like to hear those little birds
because then I know it's Spring.
And Spring comes after Winter,
surely all of this we know.
And Spring is really coming,
it's just so goddamn slow.

I am sitting by my window;
I am thinking of my rent.
I am looking through my pockets
and I am wondering where it went.
I am feeling like the Devil,
maybe like the Devil's wife.
I am singing for my supper.
I am singing for my life.

THE RENT SONG

two men of a city

Jackie is a spy.
He walks around the city
Uncovering the small jokes
Like the one about the flowers
For the dead man in the hallway.
At the funeral it said
"For the people in the courtyard."

Flowers from the dead
To the living.

He has large eyes
A very small mouth.
He reads in the front seat but
Collects all the details from the corner of his eye
Puts them in his pocket.

Guy has small eyes
A full mouth
Speaks full and eloquently,
Suave with long fingers.
The opposite of Jackie,

Who says his school of humor
Is far away with no classmates.
He writes his book of burials
Catches the world in his eyes.

Guy catches the world
through his lips.
Swirls it through his teeth happily
and spits it shining back.

Guy is the driver.
Jackie is the writer.

woman
in
the
window

(Age 16)

The setting is an alleyway and two windows facing each other. An old woman sits in one of them, smoking a cigarette, gazing down at the filthy concrete between the buildings. If you look farther down the alley, you can see a clearing with several backyards and a tree. She sits there, day after day, looking down or maybe once in a while talking to the two boys across the alley.

In the other apartment, I am pacing around my room. My brother, age eleven, comes in and throws himself on my bed.

"Hi! Why don't you be nice for once and do my dishes?"

"Get out of here, Matty. I'm busy. I have to interview someone over sixty for an English report."

"You could do my friend sitting there in the window."

I glance out my window. The woman is sitting there, as usual, looking far off in the distance.

"Yeah, I guess I could. She's over sixty?"

"I don't know." He goes over to the window and throws it open.

"Hi!" he yells out. The woman looks startled, then smiles a big smile and waves.

"Hi!" she answers.

"Yeah, that's my friend," my brother says to me. "Do you know what her name is?"

"No, what?"

"Elmer Fudd."

"What!"

"Do you know what she has for dinner every night? Rabbit stew! I'm going to do my dishes, goodbye!"

And he runs out of the room laughing before I can catch him. So, with that as an introduction, I gathered up my notebook and pen (which wasn't even used during the interview) and, fighting stage fright and nervousness, I went over to the window myself.

"Hello!" I sat down on a stool by the window.

"Hi!"

"Uh, could I interview you for a school report?"

"What?"

I could see this wasn't going to be easy, shouting at each other over the alley but, having already started, I decided to see it through.

"Could I interview you for a school report?"

"What kind?"

Her voice was surprisingly low and raspy and she lit another cigarette.

"Well, we're supposed to find out how life was fifty years ago. We're studying history."

"Fifty years ago? What year was that? This is 1975—that would be 1925? Well, sure you can interview me—but, I don't remember much about 1925. I wasn't paying any attention to history then. I don't think I can help you much. Was there a war going on?"

"I don't think so, I don't know."

"No, no, there was no war in 1925. But, I remember World War One. I had to start school the day World War One ended. All I remember were people cheering and whistles blowing, but I was very little—I had to go straight home. That was about 1918, 1917. I remember in 1929, that was the big crash. Right after that was the Depression—you've heard of the Depression?"

"Oh, yeah!" There was a small pause.

"Franklin D. Roosevelt was President then; he closed down all the banks for a day. There were long lines of people trying to get their money. No one had jobs. Things were very bad ... this is a bad year too, but it couldn't happen again. Something like that doesn't happen twice."

"Where were you living then?"

"Oh, New York."

"What was it like ... New York then? Did they have apartments like they do now?"

"Oh, sure, they had apartments ... but I lived in a house. On the East Side."

There was another pause, while we both looked down.

"What kind of clothes did they wear then?" I asked.

Here, she brightened a bit.

"Oh, they started to cut their hair—'bobbed,' I think they call it. They also started wearing makeup; before then no one wore much—no rouge, no lipstick ... and the dresses got shorter! And the waistlines were down around the hips! When I was in high school we had to wear long pleated skirts with flat shoes. We did the Charleston and things like that—we were so silly. Are you in high school?"

"Yes. I am sixteen."

"Oh, you don't look it, you look younger. What high school do you go to?"

"The High School of Performing Arts. I major in dance."

"Oh, how nice, that's really good. There were no schools like that then. I mean, you went to dancing school, I had a friend who went to one. But, it wasn't anything like that."

Here we discussed what kind of dancing I wanted to do, whether modern or musical comedy or ballet, and then we fell into another pause.

"Did you want to be anything when you grew up?"

"Well, at first I was a model."

I was surprised.

"*You* were a *model?*"

She smiled at my surprise.

"Yes. Then I had a job. I had a wonderful job as a secretary. I thought I could make more money, and I did. As a secretary—$250 a week. For a textile company. Then they moved South and wanted me to come with them. So, I did for about a month. But, I didn't like it there. I came back here and got another job very quickly. My new boss couldn't dictate letters too good—he needed me to write them. I worked there for about ten years. It was a wonderful job until I got a stroke. I got very sick. The doctors told me I shouldn't go back to work. I smoke too much. You don't smoke, do you?"

"No."

"Are those two boys your brothers?"

"Yes."

"It's just you and the two boys?"

"No, I have a little sister, too."

"Are you the one they call Alyson?"

"No, that's my sister. I'm Suzy—Suzanne."

"My sister used to talk to the boys when she lived here, but they were so little then. That was about five years ago, she died very suddenly. She would ask them, 'What's your name?' I never see your little sister."

"Do you live alone?"

"Now, yes."

"Were you ever married?"

"Yes."

"Did you have any kids?"

"Oh, no, no. We were only married for three years. He had a heart attack. I knew his heart was bad when I married him, but I hoped he would last . . . I guess you have to take these things as they come. It was very sudden."

She gave me a little smile and lit another cigarette.

"You know, I was just listening to Dr. Norman Vincent Peale on the radio. I can't stand the way the man screams . . . I don't believe in hellfire and brimstone. I don't believe that you're sinking one moment and saved the next, you know what I mean? Are you Catholic or Protestant?"

"Neither, our family isn't religious."

"Not religious? Oh!" There was another pause. "Once, I got robbed."

"Really?"

"Yeah, they took just what was on the table. My purse, like a dope, I still leave my purse there! They took a radio, it was my boyfriend's little radio. And, the funny thing was, I was asleep through the whole thing! If I had woken up, I guess they would have killed me."

"Was this recently?"

"No."

Just then, my mother came into the room.

"Suzy, Matty said you would do his dishes for him and I need them done now."

"What! Oh, boy, wait till I get him—just a minute, Ma, I'm interviewing someone for an English report."

"Well, that's okay, my arms get cramped when I sit in one position too long. From being sick," said the woman.

"Well, thank you very much."

"I'm sorry I couldn't be much help. I didn't pay any attention to history then. I guess we had a lot different history than you do! All I remember was that after the First World War, things started to change."

"Oh, no, you've helped me a lot. Thank you again for talking to me."

She smiled and shut the window.

Her lips said the word "good-bye" and she waved.

"Bye."

"How did you like Elmer Fudd?" said my brother, sauntering in. "Shouldn't you be doing the dishes?"

"Shut up! She's a nice woman, don't call her that. And do your own dishes. I have to write up my interview."

STRAIGHT LINES

There's a sound
Across the alley
Of cold metal
Touching skin

And you can see
If you look in her window
That she has gone and cut
Her hair again

In straight lines
Straight lines

Those soft golden lights in
the morning
Are now on her wooden
floor
The wind has swept them
through the apartment
She won't need them
Anymore
Anymore
Anymore . . .

She's cut down
On her lovers
Though she still dreams
Of them at night

She's growing straight
lines
Where once were flowers
She is streamlined
She is taking the shade
down
From the light

To see the straight lines
Straight lines

She wants to cut through
the circles
That she has lived in
before
She wants to finally kill
the delusions
She won't need them
Anymore
Anymore
Anymore . . .

But there's a sound
Across the alley
Of cold metal
Too close to the bone

And you can see
If you look in her window
The face of a woman
Finally alone

Behind straight lines
Straight lines

THE MARCHING DREAM

I have dreamed that many men
Have marched across this field
I have wished that I could take each man
And hold him against the flame in my heart

I had a dream that my face was old
And all the children came to see
First they laughed and then they ran
And I slammed the door behind them

And as the tears began to rise
You climbed the stairs
You came into my room
Where I was waiting there

Now I have dreamed of all men's arms
But this time it was you
I drew the curtains and it was dim
And it was strange and it was new

I have wished that I could hear
Each secret told
By lovers in the battle
With each shade of red and gold

I have wished that I could take each man
And hold him to the flame
And read the secret writing there
And know each one by name

I have dreamed that many men
Have marched across this field
I have wished that I could pour
My life into each one
Listening
Listening
Listening

THE QUEEN AND

The soldier came knocking upon the queen's door
He said, "I am not fighting for you anymore"
The queen knew she'd seen his face someplace before
And slowly she let him inside.

He said, "I've watched your palace up here on the hill
And I've wondered who's the woman for whom we all
    kill
But I am leaving tomorrow and you can do what you
    will
Only first I am asking you why."

Down the long narrow hall he was led
Into her room with her tapestries red
And she never once took the crown from her head
She asked him there to sit down.

He said, "I see you now, and you are so very young
But I've seen more battles lost than I have battles won
And I've got this intuition, says it's all for your fun
And now will you tell me why?"

The young queen, she fixed him with an arrogant eye
She said, "You won't understand, and you may as well
    not try"
But her face was a child's, and he thought she would cry
But she closed herself up like a fan.

And she said, "I've swallowed a secret burning thread
It cuts me inside, and often I've bled"
He laid his hand then on top of her head
And he bowed her down to the ground.

"Tell me how hungry are you? How weak you must feel
As you are living here alone, and you are never
    revealed
But I won't march again on your battlefield"
And he took her to the window to see.

And the sun, it was gold, though the sky, it was gray
And she wanted more than she ever could say
But she knew how it frightened her, and she turned
    away
And would not look at his face again.

THE SOLDIER

And he said, "I want to live as an honest man
To get all I deserve and to give all I can
And to love a young woman who I don't understand
Your highness, your ways are very strange."

But the crown, it had fallen, and she thought she would
   break
And she stood there, ashamed of the way her heart
   ached
She took him to the doorstep and she asked him to wait
She would only be a moment inside.

Out in the distance her order was heard
And the soldier was killed, still waiting for her word
And while the queen went on strangling in the solitude
   she preferred
The battle continued on . . .

silver and magic

(Age 15)

silver and magic
 winged creatures with
  hair of blazing fire
spiraling into the infinite
 black sky with crimson clouds
the echoing laughter of a nightmare
a crazy woman with green
 eyes that consume
 with long amber hair
long flowing dresses
 all here is glittering
 like sunlight on water
 shimmering through the air
  over the earth
what an earth! with suns of blue and gold
 shining far away
  through the black sky
   crimson clouds . . .
Red clouds! color of blood
 and the rivers that rage are
  veins of this living earth
that sees all . . . nothing is unnoticed
  Madness reigns!
in the early morning
 she walks by the river
  lost in thought
   entangled in thought
 her green eyes would turn into herself
what would she consume then?
 but the river takes a corner of her mind
runs free with it
pulls the gnarled mass
 smooth once more
a ribbon now—no longer tangled
here she is Queen
princess of fire and diamond crystal
 but her earth understands her
and sends its blood
 so she will not destroy herself
here she is safe.

Watch while the queen
In one false move
Turns herself into a pawn

Sleepy and shaken
And watching while the blurry night
Turns into a very clear dawn

Do you love any, do you love none
Do you love many, can you love one
Do you love me?

Do you love any, do you love none
Do you love many, can you love one
Do you love me?

One false move
And a secret prophecy
Well, if you hold it against her,
First hold it up and see

That it's one side stone
One side fire
Standing alone among all men's desire
(they want to know)

Do you love any, do you love none
Do you love many, can you love one
Do you love me?

Do you love any, do you love none
Do you love many, can you love one
Do you love me?

And if you wonder
What I am doing
As I am heading
For the sink

I am spitting out
All the bitterness along with half
Of my last drink

I am thinking
Of your woman
Who is crying
In the hall

KNIGHT MOVES

It's like drinking gasoline
To quench a thirst
Until there's nothing
There left at all

Do you love any, do you love none
Do you love many, can you love one
Do you love me?

Do you love any, do you love none
Do you love many, can you love one
Do you love me?

"Walk on her blind side"
Was the answer to the joke
It's said there isn't a political bone
In her body

She would rather
Be a riddle but she keeps
Challenging the future
With a profound lack of history

Do you love any, do you love none
Do you love many, can you love one
Do you love me?

Do you love any, do you love none
Do you love many, can you love one
Do you love me?

And watch while the queen
In one false move
Turns herself into a pawn

Sleepy and shaken
And watching while the blurry night
Turns into a very clear dawn

Do you love me?
do you love me?
do you love me?
do you love me?
do you love me . . .

the abdication

take the throne
throw it home
watch it crumble
made of stone
made of dust
no trust
abdicate it
if you must

when will you stop running
from a human situation
no relation
hesitation
welcome to
the abdication

masochistic
blind fool
call me cold
call me cruel
and if you have
an invitation
welcome to
the abdication

more schizophrenic
than the next
are you confused?
read the text
sorry dear
no more tears
watch this woman
disappear

standing in the waiting room
with no one here to meet me
I was here to see some king
I've given up completely
instead I meet some joker
jester sent to try and cheat me
traveled far from the station
looking for the abdication

dinner

Once again
it is made so clear
that things are not
what they seem to be.
We are at the table,
eating humble pie.

To spit or to swallow?
You swallow if you must.
And I will show you fear
in this mouthful of dust.

The queen is ripped away
and stripped away
and sitting in the corner
revealed to be the fool.

The fool. The fool.
The little bitty fool
with the little bitty arms
trying to raise the weight
above her head.

command

As though you could
Command the silence
Itself to speak.

As though you could
Demand
From nothing
A being.
An answer.

Each word here
Carved in relief against
The background of fear.

As though you could squeeze
A living response
From a thing that you've killed.

As though your power
Could bring into being
Something not born
Something not here.

As though your rage and your voice
Could bend each piece of life
Toward your will.

Your voice, white and burnt
On the machine
Barked into the room,
and no one to receive it.

Silence to answer.

Your power raising nothing.

fact

**It's not the fist, not the
Smack, not the
Black eye
It's the unexpected
Tenderness
That makes you cry**

My name is Luka
I live on the second floor
I live upstairs from you
Yes I think you've seen me
before

If you hear something late
at night
Some kind of trouble,
some kind of fight
Just don't ask me what it
was
Just don't ask me what it
was
Just don't ask me what it
was

I think it's because I'm
clumsy
I try not to talk too loud
Maybe it's because I'm
crazy
I try not to act too proud

They only hit until you cry
And after that you don't
ask why
You just don't argue
anymore
You just don't argue
anymore
You just don't argue
anymore

Yes I think I'm okay
I walked into the door
again
Well, if you ask that's
what I'll say
And it's not your business
anyway
I guess I'd like to be alone
With nothing broken, noth-
ing thrown

Just don't ask me how I
am
Just don't ask me how I
am
Just don't ask me how I
am

My name is Luka
I live on the second floor
I live upstairs from you
Yes I think you've seen me
before

If you hear something late
at night
Some kind of trouble,
some kind of fight
Just don't ask me what it
was
Just don't ask me what it
was
Just don't ask me what it
was

They only hit until you cry
And after that you don't
ask why
You just don't argue
anymore
You just don't argue
anymore
You just don't argue
anymore

LUKA

Confession

Excuse me please I know that it is
Boring to repeat
And to repeat the tale
Again but really

What is there to do?
but to accuse
and defend
to any handy jury
the details of the crimes;
the names and dates and places
the angle of the sun.
The day within the week.
The corner of the house
Strip away the feeling
Revealing only fact
Fluidity my tactic. My strategy and plan.
Hope that all assembled faces
Can crack the code.

judge and justice and the little jury

The girl came to the door of the judge and asked him to pronounce her innocent or guilty so the laughing crowd could be appeased and would not follow her through the town streets, looking and pointing.

"See the little princess!" they said, laughing. "See how she picks through the garbage—she looks like no one here. She must be guilty!"

The judge looked her up and down and said, "Yes. Come in, my child. I remember a case like yours, where a child heard voices and tried to live true. Come in, and we will see what we can do."

She said, "I am a flower, in a garden, and I am looking only for the way, and the light. They told me to call upon the Law, and so I am here."

He took her in, and the jury had gone for the day, to the park to finish playing—they would be back by nightfall. "So." he said, and he took her to a room in the back of the courthouse. "So, we will examine your evidence, and see if you'll go free."

"You see my robe." he said. "It is as black as blindness and as deep as the night sky—" and he took her upon his knee, turned her head into his chest and drew his sleeve across her eyes. And she could not see.

"I see you have taken a vow of silence somewhere" he said, and put his hand over her mouth. "This is your crime. Now you must never tell anyone what is about to happen, for you are guilty and must do penance."

And, still in his robe, removed her clothing and rocked back and forth with her in a blizzard of stillness until she knew that she saw the stars falling in a chaos through her blindness as the order let go of them from the sky. And she knew then that there was no more Law but his.

"If you are looking for Lady Justice," he said, "she is at the park with the jury—if you are looking for a guiding hand you may as well give up, for Lady Justice sleeps with me here at night in my bed. And soon they will return. Put your clothes back on, and wash yourself off."

To the Lady and the jury he said, "She is guilty, just see the way she walks, and the way she will not talk."

To the crowd beyond, he said, "She is fine, as right as rain, do not torment her or follow her around. She was merely mistaken, and when she learns to turn around, away from her white bars with the hearts, then she will be free. She *is* free, only locked in here for a time. That is all."

I said, I am a little girl
he said, you never were
I said, I am not ready
he said, then tell me when you are
I said, I am too young for this
he said, you are not really
I said, I think I am afraid
he said, you're being silly

N O T
M E

not me
not me

I said, I do not understand
he said, you are pretending
that would seem to contradict
the message you are sending
I said, you must be lonely
he said, I would not worry
I said, I think I'm dreaming
or I'm growing in a hurry

this is not me
not me

he took somebody by the hair
and dragged her down the hall
he took her to the bathroom
where they could not hear the call
he took her to a little room
she could not find the key
but I don't know who it was because
I know it was

not me
not me

and when will you stop running
from a human situation?
he said, do you think your silences
are helping this relation?
do you think your solitude
will teach you to be free?
I said, I don't know who you're talking to
I know it is not me

not me
not me

BAD WISDOM

Mother, the doctor knows something is wrong
'Cause my body has strange information
He's looked in my eyes and knows I'm not a child
But he doesn't dare ask the right question

Mother, my friends are no longer my friends
And the games we once played have no meaning
I've gone serious and shy and they can't figure why
So they've left me to my own daydreaming

What price to pay
For bad wisdom
What price to pay
For bad wisdom
Too young to know
Too much too soon
Bad wisdom
Bad wisdom

Mother, you've taught me the laws are so fine
If I'm good that I will be protected
I've fallen through the crack and there's no getting back
And I'll never trust whoever gets elected

Mother, your eyes have gone suddenly cold
And it wasn't what I was expecting
Once I did think that I'd find comfort there
And instead you've gone hard and suspecting

What price to pay
For bad wisdom
What price to pay
For bad wisdom
Too young to know
Too much too soon
Bad wisdom
Bad wisdom

Mother, I'm cut at the root like a weed
'Cause there's no one to hear my small story
Just like a woman who walks in the street
I will pay for my life with my body

What price to pay
For bad wisdom
What price to pay
For bad wisdom
Too young to know
Too much too soon
Bad wisdom
Bad wisdom

song of the black dress

Somewhere in
The inner house
The girl is standing still.
Still standing in the doorway
In her mother's dress.
The dress is black
It's made of lace
Ripped and torn along the hem.
The only way to make it fit.
Tear the dress
And rip the girl.

Lolita
Almost grown
Lolita
Go on home

Hey, girl
Don't be a dog all your life
Don't beg for
Some little crumb of affection

Don't try
To be somebody's wife
So young
You need a word of protection

LOLITA

Lolita
Almost grown
Lolita
Go on home

Hey, girl
I've been where you are standing
Leaning in the doorway
In your mother's black dress

So hungry
For the one understanding
Looking for a token of
Blood or tenderness

Lolita
Almost grown
Lolita
Go on home

Lolita . . .

THOSE WHOLE GIRLS (RUN IN GRACE)

Those whole girls
Hurl down words
Run in packs
With bloom to spare

They know health
Know it well
Skim the cream
And fill the brim

Drip with news
Spin intact
Blaze and stun
And feel no lack

Breathe with ease
Need no mercy
Move in light
Run in grace

Run in grace
Run in grace
Run in grace

you said, come with me
and so I did
I thought I could take
all your sorrow
I thought I could hold it all
I never imagined
your oceans
so bitter
the killing
the falling
the slaughter
of feather and bone.

I sat still
in the five o'clock light
the sun came in through the crack
the floor to your room
was all splinters
and, still,
some are remaining
through skin
and through flesh
cutting in patterns
like diamonds
like needles
down to the bone.

FEATHER
AND
BONE

I had to know
I had to see
I can take it all
but I will learn
to be free

I loved you
more than you'll ever know
even through broken windows
through the blood as it
ran down your fist
even
though it was my life
and my truth
and my hope
and my window gone.

and now
if you think I'm
coming back home
first I should tell you a secret.
I sleep with a sword near my hand
each night
sharpened with dreams
of your body
your murder
your blood
as it runs down
my street.

very fine laws

I have heard that your laws are very fine
Very strong and right
I'm afraid they don't do much
For me.

For chaos has a sneaky hand
To reach between the rules
If you don't believe me, just
Go look out the window.

Here is the victim's face.
I know you don't like to see it.
Why not cover it, then
With a pillow, for example?

All of us fall through the cracks
Through the slippery fingers
Of your fine and righteous laws
You may as well join us
Down here laughing.

italy in spring

The city is made of marble,
of stone. Where history lies
in castles by the water.
The people dress in wool,
and in leather, and in silk,
in ivory, brown and green.

"Who do you speak for?"
he said to me.

"The man in the corner
with the wish to be free.
The girl with no voice,
and no choice against the hardened language.

"The person in the cell
with the window so high
that you fall to your knees
if you want to see the sky."

Excuse me
If I may
Turn your attention
My way

One moment
I won't plead
It isn't much
It's what I need

And what's so small to you
Is so large to me
If it's the last thing I do
I'll make you see

If you turn from me
You darken my sun
You snap that thin thread
I call my horizon

And I'd like to remind you
Of something small
That the rock in this pocket
Could cause your fall

And what's so small to you
Is so large to me
If it's the last thing I do
I'll make you see

I might be out like a light
Extinguished in the throw
But I'll hit my mark
And you'll know

Because I'm really well acquainted
With the span of your brow
And if you didn't know me then
You'll know me now
You'll know me now

And what's so small to you
Is so large to me
If it's the last thing I do
I'll make you see

So small to you
And so large to me
If it's the last thing I do
I'll make you see
Make you see
Make you see

ROCK IN THIS POCKET (SONG OF DAVID)

If you were to kill me now right here
I would still look you in the eye
And I would burn myself into your memory
as long as you were still alive

I would live inside of you
I'd make you wear me like a scar
And I would burn myself
into your memory
and run through everything you are

I would not run
I would not turn
I would not hide

IN THE EYE

I would not run
I would not turn
I would not hide

In the eye

If you were to kill me now right here
I would still look you in the eye
And I would burn myself
into your memory
as long as you were still alive

I would not run
I would not turn
I would not hide

anti-hero

I smash my head against this
world
Until I understand it.

I would not run
I would not turn
I would not hide

I promise you I'm in this for
the long run.

In the eye

Kafka was a roach
Dostoevsky a mouse
I am a fly on the wall of this
place.

Look me in the eye

Buzzed and dumb
but learning to speak.
I'll buzz and goad
Until you hear
my small voice
and reason for being.

WHEN HEROES GO DOWN

**When heroes go down
They go down fast
So don't expect any time to
Equivocate the past**

**When heroes go down
They land in flame
So don't expect any slow and careful
Settling of blame**

**I heard you say
You look out for the feet of clay
That someone will be falling next
Without the chance
For last respects
You feel the disappointment**

**When heroes go down
Man or woman revealed
You can't expect any kind of mercy
On the battlefield**

**I heard you say
You look out for the feet of clay
That someone will be falling next
Without the chance
For last respects
You feel the disappointment**

**When heroes go down
Man or woman revealed
Do you show any kind of mercy
On the battlefield?**

**When heroes go down
When heroes go down
When heroes go down**

MEN IN A WAR

Men in a war
If they've lost a limb
Still feel that limb
As they did before

He lay on a cot
He was drenched in a sweat
He was mute and staring
But feeling the thing
He had not

I know how it is
When something is gone
A piece of your eyesight
Or maybe your vision

A corner of sense
Goes blank on the screen
A piece of the scan
Gets filled in by hand

You know that it was
And now it is not
So you just make do with
Whatever you've got

Men in a war
If they've lost a limb
Still feel that limb
As they did before

If your nerve is cut
If you're kept on the stretch
You don't feel your will
You can't find your gut

And she lay on her back
She made sure she was hid
She was mute and staring
Not feeling the thing
That she did

I know how it is
When something is gone . . .
(Repeat to end)

caecescu's army

March them to the goal.
Harness up the soul.
Don't let them dream
Or even stop to think
About the toll.

Hand picked. Hand raised.
Army made of orphans.
Strut them down the long façade.
Teach the child to fear the rod.

No indecision here.
Only precision here.

Institution green
The walls are cracked and dim
And we are standing in a line
Waiting for our faces to be seen

Institution green
Watch the floor and count the hours
None will meet my eyes
Private people in this public place

I wonder if they'll take a look
Find my name inside that book
Lose me on the printed page
Where to point the aimless rage

I cast my vote upon this earth
Take my place for what it's worth
Hunger for a pair of eyes
To notice and to recognize

Institution green
A woman stands behind a table
She will call my name
After that I'll be admitted in

I wonder if she'll take a look
Find my name inside that book
Lose me on the printed page
Where to point the aimless rage

I cast my vote upon this earth
Take my place for what it's worth
Hunger for a pair of eyes
To notice and to recognize

Institution green
Teach me how to pull the lever
Push the curtain closed
Take what's needed then just
Let me go

INSTITUTION GREEN

PRIVATE
GOES
PUBLIC

Smile no smile
On this face today
Jerk like a thing on a string
And go join the parade

Code will keep your privacy in
It won't help to win friends
Influence strangers
Or otherwise be in the swim

Mask will keep your features in check
'Cause face is the place
Where the private goes public
And steps through the gate

Take your last kick now
At any regime
Smile no smile
See if they see what you mean

Da da da . . .

thoughts

For so many years
I believed what he said
Politics was it
and religion was dead.

A guiding hand
in a private place
was the price to pay
for an innocent face.

Now it's a private rage
on a public stage
How to release
the door of the cage?

WOMAN ON THE TIER
(I'LL SEE YOU THROUGH)

(Adapted from *Dead Man Walking* by Sister Helen Prejean)

Too hot. No air.
Loud fan and a big tin can.
Wait here. Steer clear.
They've gone to get your man.

Ten A.M.
Through gate three with a picture ID.
This old billfold
Experiences security.

I hear the click. These men are hard.
I'll see your face through bar and guard.
You're new to me. I'm new to you.
I see your fate. I'll see you
You through.

Ice within.
It's all cement in the government.
Approved? Then move
To the plywood booth where the prisoner's sent.

You read in red
The letters on the door and you know what they're for.
You feel unreal.
And the rattling chain's coming over the floor.

I hear the clock. These walls are green.
I see your face through tin and screen.
You're new to me. I'm new to you.
I see your fate. I'll see you
You through.

Too hot. No air.
Loud fan and a big tin can.
Wait here. Steer clear.
They've gone to get your man.

B1G SPACE

He said you stand in your own shoes
I said I'd rather stand in someone else's
He said you look from your direction
I said I like to keep perspective

Close to the middle of the network
It seems we're looking for a center
What if it turns out to be hollow?
We could be fixing what is broken

Between the pen and the paperwork
There must be passion in the language
Between the muscle and the brain work
There must be feeling in the pipeline

Beyond the duty and the discipline
I know there's anger in a cold place
All feelings fall into the big space
Swept up like garbage on the weekend

Between the pen and the paperwork
There must be passion in the language
Between the muscle and the brain work
There must be feeling in the pipeline

All feeling
Falls into the big space
All feeling
Swept into the
Avenues of angles

Between the pen and the paperwork
I'm sure there's passion in the language
Between the muscle and the brain work
I know there's feeling in the pipeline

SONG OF SAND

(Adapted from *Woman in the Dunes* by Kobo Abe)

If sand waves were sound waves
What song would be in the air now?
What stinging tune
Could split this endless noon
And make the sky swell with rain?

If war were a game that a man or a child
Could think of winning,
What kind of rule
Can overthrow a fool
And leave the land with no stain?

tears

When the white bird
Comes beating up in my breast
Blinding and blurring my eyes
With its hot white feathertips
I beat it down.
And when it rises again
In its white hot flurry
I will snap its little neck.
                    Don't cry.
                    Don't scream.

hiroshima

people made chains
of the paper cranes
laid them down at the steps
of the stones and statues

the land was burned
this land was bare
we cannot know what
happened there

how a shadow of a human
was burnt into stone

but life took root
and something grew
no thanks to you or me

it takes root in us though
and for this we thank.

FAT MAN
AND
DANCING GIRL

I stand in a wide flat land
No shadow or shade of a doubt
Where the megaphone man
Met the girl with her hand that's
Covering most of her mouth

Fall in love with a bright idea
And the way a world is revealed to you
Fat man and dancing girl
And most of the show is concealed from view

Monkey in the middle
Keeps singing that tune
I don't want to hear it
Get rid of it soon

MC on the stage tonight
Is a man named Billy Purl
He's The International Fun Boy
And he knows the worth of a beautiful girl

Stand on the tightrope
Never dreamed I could fall, well

Monkey in the middle
Keeps doing that trick
It's making me nervous
Get rid of it quick

I stand in a wide flat land
No shadow or shade of a doubt
Where the megaphone man
Met the girl with her hand
That's covering most of her mouth

Does she tell the truth?
Does she hide the lie?
Does she say it so no one can know?
Fat man and the dancing girl
And it's all part of the show, you know?

Stand on the tightrope
Never dreamed I could fall, well

Monkey in the middle
Keeps singing that tune
I don't want to hear it
Get rid of it soon

Monkey in the middle
Keeps doing that trick
It's making me nervous
Get rid of it quick

We're all in one wide field
We thought there was no end
Walking as the field went dry
What did we do then?

We're all in one wide place
Burning every leaf and bough
Watching as the field goes dry
And what do we do now?

And what do we do now?

ONE WORLD (FOR ONE WORLD ONE VOICE)

And so you wrote
and said you had a story
called In the Flat Field
and it wasn't any good.

What I'd like to know is
what kind of field it was.
a magnetic field?
an emotional field?
or a wheat or a cotton field?

in the flat field

A barren field in winter?
or one already done
with growing for the year?
Why were you standing?
what were you looking for?
and did you find anything?

Reason I'm asking—
I'll tell you about my flat field.
As flat as a desert
twice as long and dry
I will be forever marching
looking for the limits
hoping there's something
underneath.

In the flat field
with nothing hidden.
No shade or shelter,
one stripped land.
No hiding here,
No relief.

LEONARD COHEN
interviews suzanne vega

Leonard Cohen: Alone at last. This is the first time we've ever been alone in a room together.

Suzanne Vega: Is that really true? Yeah, I guess it is true.

C: I met you first at the photographer's.

S: Right, so it was you and me and that woman.

C: And assistants.

S: ...and assistants ...

C: ...and well wishers, and onlookers.

S: Right. Then we went for a drink.

C: But, that was a public place.

S: ...that was a public place.

C: And what was the next time we met?

S: At the Juno Awards.

C: You were very kind to come to the Juno Awards and sing a fragment of my song.

S: I was very happy to come and sing a fragment of your song.

C: That was very, very kind of you. But, you could hardly say that was a private occasion.

S: Right. No, it wasn't a private occasion.

C: Our circumstances were different also. Your life has changed radically since then.

S: Well, I guess it has. I suspect yours has, although I don't know how, you know. Oh, you know because I wrote to you and told you, that's why.

C: Yes. I consider the letter very sweet, and I was touched by the fact that

you would inform me about your situation. May I apologize for not
responding.

S: Oh, no problem.

C: I myself have been in the midst of a creative struggle of some dimen-
sion. But, our lives have changed radically since that last hurried meeting in
many crowded places in Vancouver.

S: Yes, I guess it was Vancouver.

C: Now we find ourselves ...

S: But I did receive your Christmas present.

C: Oh good. What was it?

S: It was the dates that you sent through the mail.

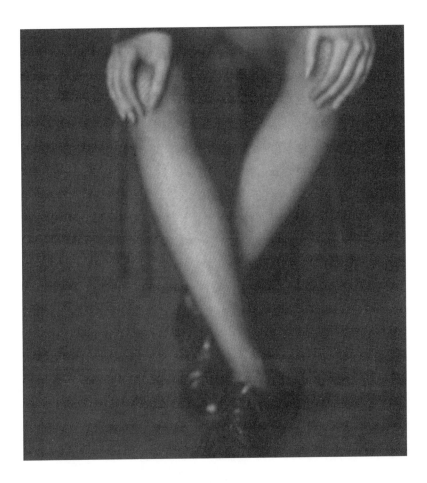

C: I'm so glad that you got those. Did you not get a little gift from me after the Juno?

S: Of course I did and I thanked you for it too.

C: Oh, good. I'm glad you thanked me for it. And did you like the dates?

S: Yeah, I liked the dates. I liked them the year before that too.

C: I hope I'll be able to send you a box of dates every year at Christmas, until circumstances really change and that extravagance can no longer be supported.

S: So, about your new album . . . no, I was kidding.

C: I've been reading the lyrics of your new album, which your management has kindly furnished me. I've been listening to the album under many circumstances. I've been listening to it in the car, with the sunroof open and closed. It sounds very, very different. The bass disappears when you open the sunroof.

S: Oh, really?

C: ...in the sound system in my car, no flaw in your record. In fact, if I may say so, the low notes, not that you sing but that are played ...

S: ...yes ...

C: ...are very, very beautiful.

S: and low, and ...

C: There's a wonderful lowness. There's a wonderful lowness about your record.

S: I feel this too, actually. We got very low to do this record.

C: I don't think you ever had anything quite this low in your previous work, the sounds ... bass sounds ...

S: It's the bass sounds, but also in the attitude I think in keeping what might normally be discarded. Keeping all of it, the distorted parts and the noise that someone else might throw away. We kept it.

C: Why?

S: There's a low sort of attitude.

C: Were you feeling reckless?

S: Yeah, I suppose I was feeling rather reckless. I was feeling like ... I mean, I have no complaints with any of my previous records, but I felt that it was all very clean and some of the things I write about are not especially clean. Art is kind of low and dark and so I felt that it was time to incorporate some of that into the music. I think that's probably why I picked Mitchell Froom to make the album. He has a taste for those kind of things.

C: It's very, very successful, and your voice against some of those moments is very beautiful, very pure. But are you as pure in your own life, in your own views as the singer presents herself? There's an austerity and a kind of unstrident idealism about the record, that is as if somebody has kept something, kept some flame alight, kept something unsullied. That's a feeling that runs through the record. Is that so in your life? Do you lead a life that is guarded?

S: I might say I lead a guarded life, yeah. I mean it's not as pure as it might look, but it's not ... it's pretty guarded. I think it's guarded because it's had to have been guarded. It's because I came from places that were not very pure and I suppose that's why I felt I needed to keep certain things clear and straight. But still I feel myself to be of the world and looking at things that are real and things that are not pure. I don't feel that I judge other people, but I judge myself very strictly.

C: You are a strict person, and others too I imagine you judge quite strictly. Except the people you happen to fall in love with. Then I imagine you make, as you say in one of your songs, in your song "In My Movie ..."

S: "If You Were In My Movie."

C: "If You Were In My Movie," in that song you seem to indicate that you would give wide allowance to anyone you fall in love with.

S: I don't know if that's true, maybe, probably. I don't know.

C: Is that what the song is about?

S: The song is about flirting. It's a flirting kind of song. It's a song looking at another person and saying these are qualities that you could be, that you could have within you. These are the things that I see.

C: You could realize these things with me.

S: Yeah, if you wanted to. It's putting a glamorous light on someone's character. Saying these are the things that, when I look at you, these are the things I see. It's like taking someone's basic nature and making it more than it actually is.

C: You have managed to make austerity extremely seductive. There is a very seductive quality about your record, although nothing is given away, nothing is thrown away, nothing is revealed.

S: Except in the artwork, where you can see my legs.

C: I haven't seen . . . nobody showed me any artwork.

S: Well, I'll have to show . . . when we're done with the interview, I'll show you the artwork. But, in that one I'm dressed as one of the characters on the album, the character of the dancing girl, and so, I'm wearing a dancing girl outfit and you can see my legs. But, I'm still wearing men's shoes and I'm wearing a cardigan sweater. So, I suppose you're right because there isn't anything being revealed, although it's hinted at.

C: It's into . . . I mean there is nothing in the record that rejects anything that is going on in this world. It casts quite a cold eye on the things around you, but there is a flirtatious—not flirtatious, I wouldn't use that word. There's a very seductive quality to all your attitudes, especially the most restrained of them. I think that's the genius of the album, behind the very careful construction of the songs and the very sparse lyrics there is some kind of raging appetite. I heard you once on the *Howard Stern Show*.

S: Oh, you did?

C: Yes, it was one morning a few months ago.

S: Oh really. Do you happen to remember what he was discussing specifically?

C: Well, I think he was discussing your breasts.

S: Yeah, I remember that day.

C: And, he seemed to be pleased.

S: He did seem to be pleased, I remember that.

C: He seemed to be pleased for one reason or another.

S: Right.

C: But the thing that pleased me about the interview, of course, next to the astounding information that Howard Stern imparted to us all . . .

S: Right.

C: . . . About your anatomy, was just the sound of your speaking voice. . . . Were you surprised at the fact that many people love you?

S: I'm surprised at it, yeah, if you put it like that. It makes me feel shy.

C: Did you not expect to be loved so widely?

S: I don't think I expected to be understood. Whether I expected to be loved . . .

C: I don't understand you. What kind of understanding have you . . .

S: I'm surprised when people understand as much as they do of the songs, because I guess I don't reveal a lot about the specific topics. You know when people say, "Well what's your message?" I never feel that I'm just revealing a message. I guess I felt if I was going to do that I could write out a message on a pamphlet or something and pass it around, and that would be a message of a kind, but it doesn't seem to be the way to do it that makes the most sense to me.

C: Well, I think that you are revealing something. There's something in the most refined and abstracted way flirtatious about the way that you refuse to reveal anything.

S: Well, I think it's because the things that attract me in real life are the things that are not obvious and the things that are not simple.

C: But do you have a kind of passion for this thing that cannot be said? May I ask you to read, would you mind reading?

S: No, I wouldn't mind.

C: For instance, the lyric of the "...Dancing Girl"

S: Okay. This song is called "Fat Man and Dancing Girl."

C: Oh, I thank you so much for reading that. I think that it has ... I think that we should study it, a little.

S: Oh yeah?

C: ...carefully. I did study this song with my son, and we went through the lyric line by line.

S: Your son, Adam?

C: My son, Adam. I would love to have the opportunity to study it with you. Because, well for one thing, I think it's a very, very beautiful, beautifully executed song on the album. I think that there are lines in it that get right to the heart of your operating mode, and I'd really like to see what I could uncover for myself and for the listener. So, let's begin at the beginning and please forgive me if I question you in what seems to be insane detail.

S: Well, I might just say, "Well, I just can't tell you that."

C: That's fine. I think that our friendship will survive this examination.

S: Okay.

C: The first line that I really would like to ask you about is this line, "and most of the show is concealed from view." What is the show that is concealed from view?

S: The way I was thinking of it was almost like a shadow puppet; the thing that is really causing the shadow is the thing that's behind the screen. But, that's not really answering your question. "Most of the show is concealed from view," meaning the real life no one sees. It's the thing that happens when I go home, or when I think about my own life or when I think about other people's lives. The thing that is the most interesting about people is the way they are when no one is looking at them or the way they are when they're in private.

C: Well, what do you see in this world?

S: And to me that is the kind of show that I give. I don't give a glamorous show. I don't come on stage in costumes or outfits.

C: Oh, I see what you mean.

S: Although, in this particular song, I'm playing at being the dancing girl. But, when I say, "most of the show is concealed from view," the real heart of the whole show is the thing that I don't do onstage. It's the private part.

C: So the resonance in your voice, the activity that your lyrics point at, is the real song?

S: Yes.

C: And it's a kind of brush painting, where a line or two will indicate a horizon, or a sky, or a sea, or a mountain, and it's just done with one or two strokes. I accept that as a partial explanation, but it's too insistent this record, the lyric is too insistent. Song after song you seem to indicate there's something going on behind the curtain, as in "As Girls Go." You say that if you could just run that number yourself and you could see behind the other side of the curtain you'd understand the situation. But, there is something that is whispering to you and something whispering to the listener all through the record. You don't have to hear it this way, you could just tap your foot to the record. It's a great record. But, for those of us that like to torture ourselves in other realms . . .

S: Yes.

C: . . . and those of us who are compelled to do interviews with imperial intentions in the middle of an afternoon these are the thoughts that assail us, there is something whispering to you, and it's something menacing. It's something . . .

S: . . . dark

C: . . . something fertile, it's something wet. It's something sexual, it's something violent. What is it really?

S: Well, it's different things in each of the songs. It's different things in each of the songs, in the place that you mentioned about what goes on behind the curtain. In that song it's wondering how far did this person take their own wish to be somebody else. You know, that's a song about a woman, by all appearances she's a woman except that you know she's a man. So you see someone like this who seems very rare. This one particular person had a very rare quality which you could kind of understand after you realized what her situation was. But, it didn't explain everything. It just made her extremely attractive and so you felt yourself drawn into her because of this rare quality and then you start to wonder how far did the whole thing go. How much pain does this person put themselves through in order to present this extremely attractive appearance, this extremely graceful and beautiful appearance? So that was my question. I mean, I never found out the answer. I didn't need to know the answer. It was more just the way this person was alluring.

C: How much pain do you go through to present this extremely attractive, modest, and refined appearance?

S: I think I've experienced a fair amount of pain in my life, but I don't feel that that's a part of the show really.

C: You have a clear idea of what the show is?

S: Yeah, I know myself pretty well. I know what my own history has been.

But, I don't feel that I need to, you know, I take parts of it and make things out of it. And mix it with other things that I know and things that I see. How much pain do I put myself through? I don't know. I mean, I have to say that at this point in my life I'm happier than I've ever been.

C: How come?

S: 'Cause I feel really free, I think, for the first time in my whole life. I think I feel very much like myself and not concerned with proving something to someone or . . . I feel like some of those more idiosyncratic parts are starting to come out now in a way that I would not have allowed before.

C: You have money, fame, youth, beauty, talent. That's a good start . . . for feeling good.

S: Yeah, but you know that doesn't mean that people are happy if they have those things. I stick to my original theory.

C: Which is?

S: Which is that I feel very free right now. I feel very happy with myself, with my own character as it is. And those other things are good, and . . . I'm not working a day job. I'm really happy about that. But I don't feel that it's these other things that have made me feel the way I've been feeling.

C: Do you have many admirers?

S: I have some.

C: I imagine they are legion. Would you please tell me what this means, "monkey in the middle keeps singing that tune, I don't want to hear it, get rid of it soon."

S: Well, the "monkey in the middle," first of all, in order to describe a song like this you have to describe the landscape it's taking place in.

C: Well, we have all the time in the world.

S: Okay. The "wide flat land" is obviously not a real land. It's a land in someone's mind or it's a land you might see in one of Picasso's paintings. You know, like the Harlequin series. It's a circus atmosphere, but it's like a bad dream or like a nightmare.

C: It's too real?

S: Too real? No, I said surreal. So in this landscape you have ... what "monkey in the middle" meant to me was that there was a person in my life who was telling me something over and over again that I didn't want to hear. I kept trying to get rid of the thing this person was saying, 'cause I felt this person wasn't understanding.

C: A real person in your life you mean?

S: Yeah, it was a real person in my life. But, within this landscape she became the monkey in the middle and I kept trying to get rid of it ...

C: She's a voice in your mind and she belongs to a real person and the things she said disturbed you deeply or inhibited you or prevented you from acting freely?

S: The thing that this woman said was ... she was warning me of something, to be careful of something. I didn't feel like being careful, and in the end she was right and I was wrong. The monkey, the tune was the one I finally heard.

C: That's a warning voice.

S: Yeah, yeah.

C: And you found that her warnings were well ...

S: Accurate.

C: ... well conceived.

S: Yeah, well conceived. 'Cause there are certain areas where I'm not cautious, where I just go tumbling headfirst and I think sometimes, in this case her advice was, yeah, well conceived. But, each of these characters is someone in my life and I wouldn't feel comfortable telling you who the different people are.

C: No, no, I know.

S: But, there's a function to each one. The megaphone man is the opposite of the girl with the hand over her mouth. The megaphone man is a person who gives information to the world. The girl who is covering her mouth is the girl with the secret, it's the same girl that's in all the songs. It's the same girl . . .

C: She has a secret?

S: Yeah.

C: It's a delicious secret sometimes.

S: Could be.

C: Or a dark secret.

S: It's a dark one. It's probably no different than the same secret every woman has. Based on that . . .

C: What is the secret that every woman has?

S: Well, I'm sure you would know.

C: I don't.

S: I'm sure you've experienced it several times, over and over again in your life. It's probably nothing more or less than that, except that sometimes it's dark, sometimes it's violent, sometimes it's stuff that you knew too early that you shouldn't have known.

C: That's another theme in this record, or at least in one of the songs, two of the songs, that there is something you find out too early. Now I don't mean to be tedious with this emphasis on this secrecy but not everybody writes every song about something that happens offstage, about something that is concealed, about a secret that is not told, not whispered.

S: Do you think every song is about this?

C: It appears in a number ...

S: In a number.

C: ... of the songs. It's a strong theme in the record, and that's why I'm just poking around trying to find out what this is. Not what the secret is but what your devotion to the secret is and how it became in a certain sense the aesthetic irritation around which the pearl of the song formed. It's something that seems to be very present in your psyche, this notion that there's something to be concealed, something to be discovered, something not quite heard, something not quite understood, something glimpsed behind the veil. It seems to be there over and over again and forgive me for trying to uncover something which has been so deliberately concealed.

S: Well, I understand your reasons for it, but I suppose in the long run, it's become the way I prefer to work because there's something beautiful in it to me. There's something beautiful in presenting it that way with the whole mystery about it intact. I think the kind of writing that I always loved was the kind of writing that had all the complications in it and everything was not explained completely. You have to say the same thing about your own work. You don't reveal everything, relationships are not always clear. There's a lot of specific things that are hinted at and you fill in the rest with your imagination but you don't come out and blurt out the sort of obvious arithmetic of it. You don't come out and say, "Well, I loved you and you don't love me," although maybe you have said that.

C: I say it over and over again, I thought. Incidentally, there is very little ...

S: Which is why I was attracted to your music at a very early age, it explained, to me it had the world the way I knew it. It didn't try and make it simple, it didn't try and clear it up for everyone. It kept it as murky as it actually is in life, and that to me is what I like about it.

C: What did you learn too early?

S: I learned about the way people can treat each other and the way people, in extreme circumstances, will do things that they wouldn't do if they were thinking about it; how people, at a very basic level, will fight to survive and act in ways that humans would prefer to not think of themselves acting like. Those are things I think I learned pretty early. That was my sense of the world, as a place where ... the world I grew up in was a very extreme place, it seemed to me. Maybe it was just because of my temperament. I don't think so. I don't think it was because of my temperament. I think it was the circumstances. Those were the first things I think I learned. I mean, I learned other things as well, but those were the things I learned too early. The other things I learned were things that children know, which are things of the imagination and things, you know, more spiritlike things. Things like, mythlike things. Those are things I also knew as a child.

C: What is the mystery of that poem ["As a Child"]? Would you mind reading it? I think it's a wonderful song. I listen to your songs in the car, with the sunroof open and closed, and listening to it in a room, and listening to it in the bath, and I find it has the quality of allowing you to leave the song and go off into your own considerations, of your own predicament where it becomes a kind of score, a kind of background for your own speculations. And I found myself, after I allowed myself to relax with the record beyond all the implications and obligations of the interview that I knew I would have to do, I tried to expose myself to the record in the normal fashion and I found that you could drift away a lot of the time, which I think is the test for music that I like. You're very polite in this record.

S: Am I?

C: In fact, you are a very polite person.

S: I think I probably am a polite person. It's gotten me in trouble many times.

C: Really?

S: Yeah.

C: That's a curious world in which courtesy and good manners now gets people in trouble.

S: Well, it did. For example, you have to imagine, say, if someone is in the ocean and they're drowning, it would be very bad. This is something that actually happened to me when I must have been twelve or thirteen, and I felt myself suddenly way over my head, and I found myself saying, "Excuse me please, but do you think you could come over here and take me out of this water because I think I'm drowning." And you know you say it in this perfectly reasonable . . .

C: Instead of screaming out, "Help!"

S: . . . instead of going, "Help!" yeah. It's the kind of thing . . . that's the kind of thing I mean. I would either prefer to swim to a shallower place by myself or somehow politely engage someone else in this life-to-life activity.

C: You thought that help would violate this sacred space between people that must at all times be preserved, this secrecy, this restraint.

S: I don't know what it was, I just felt really foolish. By the time I got out my fingernails were purple. I thought, Well that was really stupid. I thought to myself, Why didn't you just say "help?" Why didn't you just shout? And go "Help!" And it is a polite record, and it is a strange way of threatening someone, this song here. To say "Excuse me, if I may, turn your attention my way" is a terribly polite way of saying I'm going to kill you with this rock.

C: That's right.

S: So, I think you're right.

C: Who taught you these manners? Did you acquire them yourself?

S: I have no idea, my mother says I was just always like that. She says I carried myself with this way of being like a princess and even if I was going through the garbage it was always with a certain manner, which I think sometimes other people found annoying. It wasn't the kind of thing that I was taught. I have no idea where I got it from.

C: This was a style you acquired very early in your life, this kind of strong sense of the importance of maintaining the appropriate time and distance between you and the world, and you and other people.

S: It was before I was seven years old, I'd say.

C: Not to say that you reject anything, but that you have a very well-spun filter between you and the phenomena that surrounds you, for which we must be grateful because it produces these extremely mysterious and interesting songs. It is true that someone you're going to thump on the head with a rock, even if it's a small rock.

S: A small rock.

C: Is this some idea of the David story?

S: Yeah, it's some idea of it. It's a very simple version of the story of David and Goliath. It's the moment where he's trying to get Goliath's attention, you might say. Maybe Goliath in his mind is saying, Well you're too small. You're just too small for me, I can't even look at you because you're too small. David is saying, "Well, it's this small thing that can bring you down, that will cause your fall."

C: The power of the small.

S: Yeah, the power of the small thing.

C: You've mastered that, the power of the small.

S: At some point I hope to grow. It is one of the things I'm very interested in.

C: Which is?

S: That power of the small. That idea that small things have their own voice and their own will and their own life and their own dignity in the world, which is very often trampled on by people who feel they are bigger.

C: You know I was asking myself what is the essential quality of the record and the word that came to me was dignity, that it's dignified, that all your work is very dignified. That it doesn't surrender to vulgarity, that it never panders. Dignity is the quality that no matter what you're talking about you never surrender that. You never turn it into a peek show, even though you're completely concerned with this notion of curtains and concealment and what is whispered in secret, you never become coy about it. And I think that a significant achievement of your work is the dignity that it never surrenders even while talking about matters that could easily fall into an undignified confessional mode. It never even approaches that. Is this a man you're speaking to?

S: In this song? In the "Song of David"?

C: Or is it the world?

S: It's not a specific man. Sometimes I feel like it's the world. Sometimes I feel it's the way I approach the world or the audience even, I stand on the stage and I say, "Excuse me, if I may." That's the thing I want. I want their attention for that moment and somehow by the end of the show I will have made them see something. So sometimes I feel that it's my way of approaching the world or the audience, sometimes it's a way of approaching someone I feel to be bigger than myself. And it's not usually a man that I'm involved with but someone that I perceive as having authority. It's a song about authority. It's a song about striving to get that authority to know you, to know a person.

C: Is this in any way a song about your life or your career, which all of us write in some kind of secret way, those songs where you say, "Look, you've underestimated me?" If you want to relegate me as a folk singer or as this particular kind of performer or this particular kind of writer, you've got the wrong idea.

S: Yeah, there's an element of that. There's an element of that kind of challenge. Definitely.

C: So, a lot of the reviewers that I've read have made some point that this record has its flirtatious element, or that you've changed, that this represents a radical change in your work or in your direction, is it so?

S: I think I've taken more chances with this record than I have with some of the others. I think stylistically it sounds different. I was not as concerned with this record as to how it would be perceived. I was more concerned with the way it felt making it and how to feel that I was expressing parts of my personality that normally I would not have brought forth, or would've tried to polish up, or would have waited till it was more perfect. But this, I didn't want to do that at this point in my life.

C: I'm surprised to hear you say that because it has an extremely polished feel, the record. It doesn't sound like an improvisation at all.

S: No, no. It wasn't even a fact of experimenting, it wasn't as though I was trying to experiment with something wild. It was more a natural letting go of things that were already in there. And it was a question of doing what was right for each song. But, it also meant that the songs themselves had more extreme kinds of moods in them than they did before. I don't know if a song like "Blood Makes Noise"—I don't know if five years ago I might have decided that song was too ugly to put on a record, 'cause there are other songs I have that I don't put on records.

C: Oh, I see. Let's look at "Blood Makes Noise."

S: I guess if I bring it up I should expect to have it discussed. It's kind of a strange way to address one's doctor. It's a little flip. It's almost condescending.

C: It's foolish if you're sick.

S: It is foolish I suppose, if you're sick.

C: Were you sick?

S: I have been sick in my life.

C: Yes? Some of the reviewers have observed that there's a lot of medical inference and vocabulary.

S: Yeah. Well, some of that is my way of amusing myself and being what I call funny. It's a very obscure kind of humor. Some of it is because I think the language of medicine is fascinating and has its own poetry in it. And some of it I think is probably 'cause when I came off the road in 1987 I was, not seriously sick, I'm really healthy, but I was anemic and I had asthma and bronchitis and stuff you get from being run down. But I think the main reason I work with these terms is because I feel that language itself is beautiful, and especially medical language is a way of talking about the body in a way that's intimate without being corny. Although I think I've probably taken it about as far as I'm going to take it. But, I do get letters from doctors.

C: So, what do they say?

S: Oh, they say that the information is very accurate and could they use the lyrics in their own texts, and ...

C: ... could they meet you?

S: One or two want to know if they can meet me. Or they want to know how do I know so much about medicine.

C: Well, how do you know so much about medicine?

S: 'Cause I'm curious about the body, I'm curious about being healthy and I like the idea of ministering.

C: There's a very beautiful line in one of your songs. I thought it was really excellent, I underlined it, "I will pay for my life with my body."

S: It's a very sad line, in the context of it.

C: What does it mean?

S: Well the girl in the song, who is a girl with a secret, feels like the woman who walks in the street. And in that way she is in some way paying for her life with her body.

C: It's a mysterious way to describe what we all do really.

S: I suppose everyone does, ultimately.

C: We all pay for our lives with our body.

S: You mean in the final end of it, it is.

C: I mean that's what we do, pay a little bit everyday.

S: Right.

C: I thought it was a very beautiful line that is very much ...

S: I mean some people are forced to pay more with their bodies than they might under other circumstances.

C: What is the "bad wisdom"?

S: The bad wisdom is exactly the things we were talking about before. The bad wisdom is knowing something before you're ready for it. It's knowing something before it's time. Before. It could be sexual knowledge. Some kids take LSD too early.

C: Did you?

S: No. Bad wisdom is when you have too much too soon. You go beyond what you're prepared to handle.

C: To me it's quite interesting how consistent the themes are in this record. Song after song we are really discussing the same song, and the same position in regards to the information in the song. Could you read this song, "Bad Wisdom"?

S: Okay.

C: You don't have to if you don't want to. I'm going to have another glass of wine. Would you like one?

S: I'll have a little bit, yeah.

C: That's the spirit.

S: I'll have wine and I'll have water.

C: The biblical beverages.

S: It sounds so much better than coke and orange juice, or one of those kinds of things.

C: It's so very stylish of you to have just wine and water.

S: Well, thank you, Leonard. It also happens to be what is available.

C: Why won't you tell me what you really know about what the bad wisdom is?

S: Because, when I write these songs I feel the important thing is that we know that they are truthful, and it doesn't matter. It shouldn't matter to you, for example. If I'm putting these words out to be judged and I want the work to be judged, then I feel everything you need to know is in the work. There's nothing you need to know about what I know. For someone to want to know, for example, how much of these songs do I . . . what are the things in my own life. To me that's out of bounds then.

C: I completely agree with you.

S: Because then someone is open to judging my character and that's not what I'm putting out, that's not what I'm displaying. I'm putting the work out because the work is the work, and the work is what I hope is beautiful and good, and the work is what will be around after I'm not here anymore. And that to me seems like the important thing. The bad wisdom is what I said. It's knowing about something too soon. In some ways, everybody has their own form of it.

C: Well, forgive me for asking you this question over and over again, but according to the instructions that this interview may be broadcast or a transcript prepared in segments of various lengths it is my intention to ask you the same question over and over again so no matter how the segments are divided the most important response to the album will be established.

S: So what question is it that you're asking exactly?

C: I forget.

S: It all depends. The answer all depends on how it's phrased and what exactly you want to know.

C: Now, obviously the primary theme of the interview is the new album. I think that we've treated that at some length.

S: I think we have too.

C: The following list of topics is illustrative only. We would like you to touch on most of the issues so as to provide the content necessary to satisfy the promotional purpose of this piece. However, during the course of your conversation, please feel free to venture in any other areas that may come up.

S: Yes.

C: So, it was not entirely without permission that I was prodding in these areas, even though I understand that your aesthetic determines that, or is a kind of curtain, the kind of curtain you speak about, beyond which the viewer is not invited to look. There is this and this alone and this is the work and it should be judged as the work by itself without any reference to the hand that created it.

S: Yeah, I know that sounds cold.

C: That's okay. I can take it.

S: It sounds cold, but it's the way I like it.

C: You like to write about anything you don't really have to write about.

S: I like to write about things that are extreme in some form. I like to write about something I feel I have to write about.

C: Do you find it hard to write?

S: Sometimes.

C: What is the hardest song on this album?

S: The hardest song on this album was "99.9F."

C: That was hard to write? And yet, it comes off effortless.

S: That was the most difficult song. That was the song I was sitting there looking in the thesaurus and the rhyming dictionary with. Looking up synonyms and antonyms for hot, cold, fever, romance, anything I could get my hands on.

C: Is this a flirtatious song?

S: Yeah. Couldn't you tell? You couldn't tell.

C: Well, I'm immune to these kinds of approaches.

S: Oh, I see.

C: I thought it was very lovely, and to repeat that phrase "ninety-nine point nine" was very fresh. Let's look at this song.

S: Okay.

C: Why did you call this the title of your album?

S: Because I felt that it described the stance of the album, which is not normal, off the norm, not wildly feverish but off the norm enough to create tension, enough to give you a dizzy, hallucinatory feeling but not so much that you feel that you're out of your mind in listening to it. It seemed slightly hotter than maybe some of my other albums. The other albums have a much cooler tone to the whole sound of them.

C: A cautious intoxication.

S: Yeah, I guess so.

C: Do you drink?

S: Yeah.

C: What do you usually like to drink?

S: Well, let's see, these days I drink gin and tonic. I drink wine or I drink cognac or I drink brandy or I drink sake. I have a bunch of things that I like to drink.

C: Do you find that a lot of people are drinking now, these days?

S: I find that most of the people I hang out with tend to drink but I think that's also because that's the kind of crowd I hang out with. I drink Jack Daniel's.

C: What are the people like in your crowd?

S: Oh god. It's a very diverse crowd, I suppose. It's not even really like a crowd, its more like a thinly, sparsely populated little gathering of forlorn and homeless people.

C: Where do they live? Is it nationwide or is your crowd more or less in one town?

S: My crowd. Some live in New York and some live in California, and some are people I used to know from the folk scene and I'm still friends with them. In the Village. And some are new friends I made last year, and there's been some pretty wild drinking going on there. Drink to six, seven, eight the next morning.

C: Among your new friends?

S: Yeah, among my new friends.

C: Your new friends drink a lot.

S: Yes, yes we do. And I drink with them.

C: Could you let us in on one of these evenings. These drinking evenings. How do they begin? What is the middle like? And what is the ending like?

S: The beginning usually means me going to pick up my sister and she comes with me, or my brother, because they all like to hang out. We're talking about a party now, not talking about an intimate social gathering, this is a party.

C: I'd really like to know what an evening where a lot of liquor is consumed . . .

S: With me it usually ends up in wild dancing.

C: Yeah? Begins early and ends late?

S: Yes. I really love to dance.

C: What music do you dance to?

S: I used to dance to your music actually, when I was younger, seventeen or so. You'll laugh at the songs I chose to dance to, they're not what you'd think of as dancing songs.

C: On the contrary, others may not think so, but you and I know what a dancing song is.

S: "So Long Maryann," or "The Avalanche Song," or "The Master Song."

C: What are you dancing to these days?

S: There's a band called Les Negresses Vertes, which is a terrible French pronunciation on my part of their title. It's almost like gypsy music. I'll dance to that. What else will I dance to? I dance to some of the new U2 albums. Sometimes I'll dance to . . . PM Dawn has a song called "Paper Doll," which I like. Or different things that come up or catch my imagination in some way.

C: And when you go out with friends, when you're with your crowd, how are people dressing in your crowd?

S: Well, I have a friend of mine who makes dresses. Her name is J. Morgan Puett. She tends to make these big linen dresses and pants, they're loose and baggy and usually made out of cotton or linen or something like that . . . they're almost peasantlike.

C: Do you wear them too?

S: Yeah, I wear them often.

C: They have pants underneath the skirt?

S: No. Either pants, which are baggy, they're like farmers' pants. See, I'll show you the artwork of the album cover and I'm wearing some of her clothes.

C: What's that?

S: That's the album cover.

C: That's the vinyl?

S: Yeah, yeah, that is the vinyl. Here, I'll show you, hold on a second.

C: Okay. Hold on everybody, Suzanne is dancing across the room.

S: These are some of her pants.

C: Oh, that's a very nice picture.

S: They're baggy and they're really cool.

C: Those are your arms.

S: Those are my arms.

C: And what is your expression?

S: This is the expression . . . I don't know. What would you describe it as? "What the hell are you looking at?" kind of face?

C: That is the extremely seductive . . . this combination of austerity and voluptuousness that your songs manage to convey. That is a refined invitation to a cautious intoxication.

S: Well, thank you, Leonard. As opposed to the other. Here, let me show you the other poster that I see lying on the floor.

C: Okay. Suzanne is now going over to get the other poster that is lying on the floor.

S: These are the fishnet stockings from the dancing girl. The dancing girl on the album is wearing fishnet stockings and these are them blown up.

C: I know. This has many resonances of self-abuse.

S: Self-abuse?

C: Yes.

S: I don't think so.

C: I think you might be making a pass at yourself in this.

S: No, Leonard, you've got it all wrong.

C: Oh, I'm sorry.

S: You've let your imagination go too far. This is my shoe. This is my shoe. This is my knee.

C: I'm sorry. I'm sorry. I'm terribly sorry. But, I think that anybody's imagination is being invited to really careen around the place.

S: Well, we'll put this one away then.

C: Yeah, please do. A man of my age should not be compelled to look at those kind of photos.

S: So anyway, those are Morgan's pants. What I started to show you were Morgan's pants, what they look like.

C: Are you choosing your intimate male partners from among the members of this crowd? Or, do they come drifting in, they belong to other crowds?

S: No.

C: . . . sometimes no crowd at all.

S: I would say no crowd at all, really.

C: Guys stumble into your life from . . .

S: No, I wouldn't say they stumble in. You know, you asked me in the beginning if I was a guarded person, and I guess I'm sort of a guarded person.

C: I thought so until I saw those fishnet stockings. That's changed things a lot. I wish I saw that at the beginning of this interview.

S: But that's a character.

C: No, I really don't think you can use that as an alibi.

S: Oh.

C: This is you in fishnet stockings, you cannot sanitize this image.

S: Oh, I didn't say I was going to sanitize it, I just said I was in character.

C: No, I'm sorry, Suzanne.

S: It's not a very clean character, but . . .

C: You're not in character at all. First of all, there's not enough showing to indicate a costume that could even indicate a character.

S: That's because you saw an isolated detail there. You haven't seen the whole context of it.

C: You mean that's just part of the poster?

S: No, the actual picture the costume is from is ... there's a real picture.

C: Yes, but when you select your hand and a fishnet stocking and nothing else, people cannot be faulted if they don't assume you're in costume.

S: Well, they would if they ... Okay, whatever. I could fault them if I want to.

C: You can do anything you want. Would you like to talk about Mitchell Froom?

S: Would I like to talk about Mitchell Froom?

C: Yes, because the production is really extremely competent and beautiful. What was his contribution?

S: Well the reason I wanted to work with him was because I could tell from his other records that he didn't approach anything in a formulaic way, and that seemed like a good thing to me.

C: Would you like to talk about the other people who worked with you?

S: Yeah, we could do that. I think that the musicians that we used on this album, besides using ... on one track we used Mike Visceglia and Marc Schulman, who are my long-term musicians that I've played with for years. But the newer musicians are Bruce Thomas, who played with Elvis Costello for ten years, he was in The Attractions, the band. Do you like Elvis Costello or do you listen to him?

C: I've listened to him a lot. He's a great singer.

S: So, I've always liked the way his band sounded. To me it's very witty and it's got a lot of interesting things about it. And Jerry Marotta played percussion and drums.

C: Do you get along well with your musicians?

S: Yeah, I do.

C: And when you tour do you feel part of a family?

S: It has felt that way sometimes, not always, but most of the time, yeah. I do, I like it, I like the atmosphere that develops.

C: You like touring?

S: I like a lot of it. The last one was a little long.

C: How many concerts did you do?

S: I did ten months.

C: Ten months on the road?

S: Ten months on the road, sometimes five shows a week.

C: How many concerts altogether did you do?

S: I don't remember.

C: Hundreds.

S: Hundreds, yeah. Well, there's fifty-two weeks in a year, ten months . . . forty weeks, but it wasn't really forty weeks, it was more like thirty.

C: Let's say thirty weeks, let's say an average of three concerts a week. . . .

S: Ninety?

C: Nine hundred. It's nine thousand concerts, I think.

S: We can study my itinerary if we want to count them. A lot, a lot, but there's a lot about it that I love. It is like a family and I get to know . . . I'm on the road with seventeen guys that I have to know about in some way or another, and know about their lives, and what's happening with their lives. Who's having problems and who's doing well, and who's just had a baby and whose mother is sick. I enjoy that kind of feeling, of getting to know people and getting to know their character.

C: And do you feel that you occupy some maternal function on the road, that you kind of hold it together with these concerns that you just mentioned? That you are the center of the family?

S: I'm definitely the center of the family. I suppose that makes it maternal. Sometimes I feel more like the figurehead of the ship, and the engine. *Maternal's* not quite the word 'cause that implies a certain coziness which is not really always there. There's still always a bit of distance and formality, but I like the atmosphere. I like staying up and drinking and playing poker and talking and that kind of thing.

C: You like that?

S: I like the feeling of being on adventure, of being on the bus overnight on a ferry and we're going somewhere, we're going to Greece or we're going to Italy and this feeling of a shared adventure.

C: You're lucky.

S: Why is that?

C: You're lucky to have this experience.

S: Do you like touring?

C: Yeah, I like it. I kind of feel like part of a motorcycle gang.

S: Yeah, I could see that.

C: What plans do you have to tour?

S: Probably early next year.

C: Do you have your band put together yet?

S: No.

C: Can I play in it?

S: What would you like to play?

C: I don't know.

S: You could sing, you could be a backup singer.

C: Congas.

S: It's like I always go see you perform, you always have two very beauti-ful women standing by you.

C: I could be one of the beautiful women standing beside you.

S: I could have you standing behind me singing.

C: Oh, that would be a great honor. What kind of live show can be expected?

S: Well, you'll come with me and we can sing duets, we can dance.

C: Oh, that would be really nice. Now your expectations and feelings about the album, we've looked into that, but I think if you would speak about your expectations . . . but really honestly about your expectations.

S: What do you mean, "but really honestly," as though I've . . .

C: It's not that I feel you've been dishonest in any sense.

S: Well that's good because I haven't.

C: No, I don't feel you've been dishonest.

S: No.

C: But there is this tantalizing and . . .

S: . . . irritating?

C: . . . irritating is not quite the word, let's say intriguing sense of secrecy that you insist on preserving.

S: I bet.

C: I'd really like to know what you expect from this album, but really deeply. Do you think that this album will bring you the lover?

S: It's possible.

C: Do you think of it as a mating call? Do you see this album as a mating call?

S: Why? Do you see it that way?

C: Yes, yes I do.

S: Do I see it as a mating call? As a mating call?

C: Yes, I see this album as an exquisite, refined mating call of one of the most delicate and refined and concealed creatures on the scene. This is the mating call of concealment. This is how secrecy woos her lover. So, do you think that this album will bring you the lover which the album calls out to?

S: Yes.

C: I do too. I really do. I think we are at last approaching the truth of the enterprise. This no doubt will not find it's way into . . .

S: I think you're wrong. I think they'll make a headline out of it in fact. But without saying any more than that, I would say, "yes."

C: I think so. I find it irresistible myself.

S: On that cheery note, that's a cheery note to end on.

C: I think so.

behind the puppets

Behind the puppets
is a man
in a room
and here is a grinning
spinning face
upon a string

I don't dance
and I don't sing

Unless I am moved to.

tightrope

I stepped out on the tightrope
Never dreaming I could fall
And now I watch the crowd as it's
Gathering below.
Some will turn away and wonder
Why a fool is dancing up so high,
Why won't she do it on the ground?

Others stand and wait beside the gate
To see if something dangerous will happen.
Others look because they think they've
Seen me here before.

Below, the horse is white and wild,
Beautiful and proud.
I'm following my calling.

Suddenly I'm thinking
There are other ways to spend some time,
But meanwhile I am up here
On a slender piece of rope,

Not sure where the end is,
I know there's no beginning
A circus girl should ride
Balancing, barebacked on a horse

And so I entertain you
Ask for your attention
A moment of your time
A minute of your life.

the dreams

Last night in Spain I saw
a child with a bloody hand
in a back street on the cobblestones.
He held it up to me and smiled.

Last night I dreamed
of a bloody sheep
hanging and defiled,
hanging from the ceiling,
slaughtered.

I saw a big fat
black city pigeon
fluffed up sitting roundly
in the corner
of the white door.
Looking into the flat gray sky,
looking at me.

Last night sleeping
I saw the bones of a tiny bird,
hanging and dancing,
living on a string,
twisting and dancing,
fighting for her life.

I dreamed of an old man
with wide eyes and a thin mouth,
who grabbed my hand
and held it tight and told me something
I couldn't hear in words.

I dreamed that another man
ripped out a piece of his lining
from his jacket
to show us his clean quilted heart,
to show us he was not guilty,
not quiet, either.

I dreamed of how we all hang
under your oppressive roof.

TIRED OF
SLEEPING

Oh Mom, the dreams are not so bad
It's just that there's so much to do
And I'm tired of sleeping

Oh Mom, the old man is telling me something
His eyes are wide and his mouth is thin
And I just can't hear what he's saying

Oh Mom, I wonder when I'll be waking
It's just that there's so much to do
And I'm tired of sleeping

Oh Mom, the kids are playing in pennies
They're up to their knees in money
In the dirt of the churchyard steps

Oh Mom, that man he ripped out his lining
He tore out a piece of his body
To show us his "clean quilted heart"

Oh Mom, I wonder when I'll be waking
It's just that there's so much to do
And I'm tired of sleeping

Oh Mom, the bird on the string is hanging
Her bones are twisting and dancing
She's fighting for her small life

Oh Mom, I wonder when I'll be waking
It's just that there's so much to do
And I'm tired of sleeping

Oh Mom, I wonder when I'll be waking
It's just that there's so much to do
And I'm tired of sleeping

sleeps in silence

She sleeps in silence
her hands across her mouth
she's dreaming of a person
whose name she won't pronounce.

She sleeps frowning
as though it is a burden, all
the sorting and unsorting of
the voices underground.

And when she wakes
she's frightened by the silence
in the room that was so noisy
in her sleep the night before.

hand of sleep

When the big dark
Hand of sleep
Comes across my eyes
I gladly go
Down to be
In the darkest part of the deep.

When he takes me by the ankle
And pulls me down
Away from the shore
I gladly go
Down to see
What he has to show.

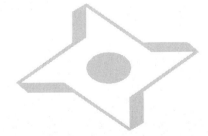

blue arabesque

Dreaming of a movie called *Blue Arabesque* about a man and his son—the son finds the father after so many years and follows him, sometimes from a distance and sometimes closely; he never gets the acceptance he looks for. One day by the river, the son takes a running start and handsprings onto the railing—his body curves in an arc, like an arabesque; the film goes blue at this point. In slow motion, in front of his father, he sails over the railing into the water. We don't know if he lives or dies.

s h a r k

anger swims beside me
like a great white fish
with small eyes and sharp teeth
patient and cool as the sea
keeping the pace
he must be mine
because he follows me

proselytizing

Let's take an ordinary experience
like snorkeling
or religious proselytizing—
and transform it into
its basic sensory experience.

Working the street.
Combing. Looking into each
Preoccupied face
For an opening.
Somewhere in this urgency
Is a true compassion.
A patience
With a big wide hand
As big as a boulder
There is my faith.
In the slow patience,
And in time
Which will crush your tyranny
More completely
Than my small fist ever could.

The urgency and hurrying
Roll off my back
Like a foam on a gray river.

snorkeling

We rode the scooters to Shoal Bay, to a crowded part of the beach. We read, ate lunch. It was uneventful until snorkeling. That was strange, surreal. To look down at the sea bed while swimming over it is like flying. Flying over an odd world that mirrors and distorts the one above—plant life waves in the currents, not the breeze, in a strange mocking imitation. Globelike plants with mazes loom in bare white stretches that look like a desert, a watery desert. Schools of fish that fly like birds, including you in their flock, unless you panic and splash, then they scatter wildly, all of them scattering in the same direction, as though dancing.

The atmosphere is moonlike and the sinewy waving plant life seems sinister—grotesque, out of proportion. Like a desert spotted with skulls too big for any body, globes, covered with mazelike paths with tiny moving fingers feeling. I think I saw a small shark. Like flying over mountains. Like dreaming.

If you get too close the tips will scrape and crunch, crush your skin and stomach—the tide swings and carries you, lulls and fascinates you until you're in the valley looking up and the hard scaly surfaces wait to grate your softness and your bone—wait to shave the surface of your body and your bone, knock your elbows and your ankles and your knees.

Your vision must be clear and your breathing should be even. We go along the tips and rocks and see the bleaching things beneath, below the rays of light like long and slender fingers picking at the fleshy things on the bottom—

A flash of color. Spot of yellow, stripe of blue. Silver. The cores and caves, hidden darker places, and open white and billowed salty plains. Dense. There aren't any breezes, only waves that lift and carry you. I feel as though I know this landscape well. And yet it's not like anything I've ever seen. Smooth. But strangely hairy. Ropey. Delicate and hefty. Floating. Sinking. Buoyant. Bobbing. Flip. And dart. Salted surfaces. Slowly stirring beneath. Rooted and stirring. Airtight. Airless.

Like flying over mountains. Or like dreaming.

The only things you must be careful of
are the tips that break the surface,
break the cushion of the water,
and poke the barrier.

And drifting from the shore
with no perspective. No direction.

CALYPSO

My name is Calypso
And I have lived alone
I live on an island
And I waken to the dawn
A long time ago
I watched him struggle
   with the sea
I knew that he was
   drowning
And I brought him into me
Now today
Come morning light
He sails away
After one last night
I let him go.

My name is Calypso
My garden overflows
Thick and wild and hidden
Is the sweetness there that
   grows
My hair it blows long
As I sing into the wind
I tell of nights
Where I could tast the salt
   on his skin

Salt of the waves
And of tears
And though he pulled
   away
I kept him here for years
I let him go.

My name is Calypso
I have let him go
In the dawn he sails away
To be gone forevermore
And the waves will take
   him in again
But he'll know their ways
   now
I will stand upon the shore
With a clean heart
And my song in the wind
The sand will sting my feet
And the sky will burn
It's a lonely time ahead
I do not ask him to return
I let him go
I let him go.

impressions of portugal

"Portugal?" says my brother. "Isn't that a totally coastal country?" he says, in that American way some people have of speaking.

Yes, it is totally coastal, I tell him. It's a total coast, with miles of beach. It's a fishing country, where fishermen still sail every day, and people cook sardines by leaning out of their windows, and grilling them on the small and winding streets in the older parts of Lisbon. I remember seeing the ocean in Portugal for the first time. It was at night, and the hotel restaurant looked out over the water. I wanted to know, what was the color? Blue or turquoise or green?

Have you never seen the ocean before? my hosts wanted to know. Of course I had seen the ocean, but never this one. I looked out at the expanse of the sea that night, and then the next morning, looking at the clear gold light of the sun over so much water, and felt the weight of the history. You feel this history in the sea—which, of course is eternal—and in the buildings. The light and the architecture combine to make beautiful sweeping views, as in old paintings—the towers and clocks against the play of clouds and sea have a rich lovely color, so different from the pale watery stark light of Germany or Northern England. These buildings were alive during the centuries following the eighth century Moorish occupation and are still alive today, although some have very modern graffiti on them. For those who are interested in this history, much of the old architecture is intact because Portugal was untouched in the two World Wars.

But besides all these weighty historical feelings, I also felt all possibilities open for the future, as though I were a kind of female Henry the Navigator surveying the avenues of exploration upon the horizon. I had the feeling if I looked hard enough perhaps I could see my apartment in Manhattan, which overlooks the Hudson River. Portugal is not mummified, or kept behind glass, self-consciously historical and prim; it is down to earth, sometimes dirty, and sometimes elegant, but always alive and friendly.

I was invited in 1988 to visit President Soares at the Palace, which surprised me, as I am not used to invitations from high places. Why? I wondered. Your album, *Solitude Standing* has done very well here—in fact you are referred to as "the girl from the radio," I was told.

I began to do some research. Did the people of Portugal like him? Would my visit provoke any protest? Yes, they liked him. No, they would not protest. He seemed to have the rare talent of being able to please both the left and the right wing at the same time—a liberal conservative of sorts. I was impressed. In my own country, all you ever heard was complaints against the government, especially in New York, and I had never known a people to be happy with their elected representatives.

The President was gracious, but neither of us spoke the other one's language. We smiled at each other a lot. I went with someone from the record company, my boyfriend, and my manager. We sat down in a line and spoke for a few minutes, had our pictures taken, and then we got up and began to mill around the beautiful palace, which looks something like a museum. Formal circumstances, even as informal as these, always make me uncomfortable, so I thought that I would initiate a movement to conclude our visit and marched forward confidently to the huge front doors and tried to throw them open.

"Oh, Miss Vega, wouldn't you rather leave through the front door rather than the second story window?" said the guard, running over to prevent me from flinging myself off the balcony. It still makes me laugh to think about it, but the President was kind, and I was pleased he took the time to invite me.

We had a press conference that night, in a small club. I told the story there, and it made the front row laugh. I had seen these same young women at the airport the day before. My memories are that I was mobbed when I arrived. The reality was probably that there were more like ten people, but I remember the photographers, and the pictures they snapped of my surprised face as we drove away in the car. They printed them with gusto the next day in the newspapers.

I had lunch with some of the journalists during my visit, which I loved, because the weather was soft and sunny, and we ate outdoors in a restaurant with painted tiles near the entrance. There were leaves overhead, and we ate fish and drank *vinho verde*. I told them I felt I was a journalist in my songs, and they responded that they felt they were artists.

Why did you write about the Portuguese women in your song "Ironbound"? they wanted to know. Because I had seen some Portuguese women in the Ironbound section of Newark, New Jersey, near where I live, and they looked very beautiful and womanly to me, and it made me feel that I was in a romantic and warm place far away, like Lisbon. When I sing that line onstage, all eight thousand people in the audience in Lisbon, or Oporto, or Cascais, cheer and scream and sing along happily. They wave their arms and celebrate.

There was one Portuguese woman who sang and played the guitar to warm up the audience for me a few times. Her name was Pilar, and she sang by herself, with no band or other accompaniment. I remember mostly her dark lustrous hair and her beautiful sad songs, and her voice that sounded ripped from her, or torn out of her. One minute her voice was caressing, and the next sad; she would croon, hiccup, cry, and accuse. It had an extraordinary effect on the audience, especially the men and boys; they howled in response. It didn't seem to matter which words she sang. They howled in response to the pure sound of her voice. I did too, within myself.

I believe that the soul of Portugal, besides being in the sea, is in the songs. I went to a small club one night, where a woman was singing unamplified in the center of the room, with her head thrown back, like she was wailing or moaning. Everyone pressed in close to hear her. This was *fado* singing, a kind of singing that began in the sixteenth century and continues today. The songs are about destiny, fate, and human passions, and are usually very sad. I understand why.

An imposing man followed her, and I heard whispers that this singer was a judge in his daily life. Again I was impressed, as in the United States you would never see a judge singing in a nightclub. Here it seemed the most natural thing. Who should sing about fate and human destiny if not a judge? As he sang, he turned around so the entire room could see him; he seemed to look in my direction and his mouth opened very wide (at me?); a tremendous sound of singing and wailing poured out of him. I felt flattened against the wall and for a moment was relieved that he was not my father, and that he had no cause to be angry with me, as I would not want to provoke such a wrath. Afterward we talked in a friendly way and he gave me one of his recordings.

The last image I have of Portugal was just before Christmas one year, when I was in our tour bus, riding through the warm streets, looking at the grocery stores with huge pieces of dried codfish hanging outside. Some of these hanging fish are as big as a man. On one street corner in front of all this fish was a man, in fact, waiting for the light to change, and casually smoking a cigarette with his hand on his hip. He was thin, and looked tired, and like he needed a shave. Perhaps this would not have made an impression, except that he was dressed as Santa Claus, and his red pants hung low around his dark narrow hips. He made no pretense of being jolly or fat or nice, and I admired him for it. Besides this I remember the faces, which to me look like those of my family, though not my own—the dark skin and the large dark eyes, the round faces and the wide cheekbones of my brothers and sister I grew up with.

in liverpool

(From the *99.9 F°* Special Package)

the bells are clanging and clamoring from what appears to be a church—now they have stopped, rung twice—now the ceremony is over—it had gone on for a good five or ten minutes. two clocks look into my hotel room and from the window I see a small brown river—is this the river Mersey that Andy A. once told me about? I thought of him today as the bus rolled into town—how homesick he was for Liverpool, for the big clock that always told the same time—where is it? for the river Mersey which, if this is it, is much smaller and browner than the Hudson, which I am homesick for right now—

the light is pale and thin here like the inhabitants of this country—a pale watery light not unpleasant but not substantial—

here the bells have started again—the ringing begins at the top of the scale and hurls itself down in a mad clamor over and over again in an uneven rhythm—

there must be some mad boy in the belfry hurling himself across the ropes like a hunchback. perhaps he loves someone who doesn't love him. perhaps he is remembering an old lost love. now the scale is confused and sounds like a carnival of bells, a dull peculiar melody, with a lilt but no reason to it.

now it returns to the scale from the beginning over and over from the top down to the bottom the low notes hitting with a dark clanging resonance, the top bells more cheerful—besides this banging and clamoring there is no other sound, no shouts, traffic, people, nothing except the stone, the pale sunlight, the small brown river, and the bells on a Sunday afternoon.

IN LIVERPOOL

In Liverpool
On Sunday
No traffic on the avenue
The light is pale and thin
Like you
No sound, down
In this part of town

Except for the boy in the
  belfry
He's crazy, he's throwing
  himself
Down from the top of the
  tower
Like a hunchback in heaven
He's ringing the bells in the
  church
For the last half an hour
He sounds like he's miss-
  ing something
Or someone that he knows
  he can't
Have now and if he isn't
I certainly am

Homesick for a clock
That told the same time
Sometimes you made no
  sense to me
If you lie on the ground
In somebody's arms
You'll probably swallow
  some of their history

And the boy in the belfry
He's crazy, he's throwing
  himself
Down from the top of the
  tower
Like a hunchback in heaven
He's ringing the bells in the
  church

For the last half an hour
He sounds like he's miss-
  ing something
Or someone that he knows
  he can't
Have now and if he isn't
I certainly am

I'll be the girl who sings
  for my supper
You'll be the monk whose
  forehead is high
He'll be the man who's
  already working
Spreading a memory all
  through the sky
In Liverpool
On Sunday
No reason to even remem-
  ber you now

Except for the boy in the
  belfry
He's crazy, he's throwing
  himself
Down from the top of the
  tower
Like a hunchback in heaven
He's ringing the bells in the
  church
For the last half an hour
He sounds like he's miss-
  ing something
Or someone that he knows
  he can't
Have now and if he isn't
I certainly am

In Liverpool
In Liverpool

waterfront town

The bellhop boy
with the long thin face
the short-cut hair
the angular grace

Mentions to you that
he's looking for a place
As he takes you to your room . . .

ROSEMARY

Do you remember how you walked with me
down the street into the square?
How the women selling rosemary
pressed the branches to your chest,
promised luck and all the rest,
and put their fingers in your hair?

I had met you just the day before,
like an accident of fate,
in the window there behind your door.
How I wanted to break in
to that room beneath your skin,
but all that would have to wait.

In the Carmen of the Martyrs,
with the statues in the courtyard
whose heads and hands were taken,
in the burden of the sun;
I had come to meet you
with a question in my footsteps.
I was going up the hillside
and the journey just begun.

My sister says she never dreams at night.
There are days when I know why;
those possibilities within her sight,
with no way of coming true,
'cause some things just don't get through
into this world, although they try.

In the Carmen of the Martyrs
with the statues in the courtyard
whose heads and hands were taken,
in the burden of the sun;
I had come to meet you
with a question in my footsteps.
I was going up the hillside
and the journey just begun.

All I know of you
is in my memory.
All I ask is you
Remember me.

watertown: a journal

In 1982 I was working a day job, as I often did. In my life I have been: a baby-sitter, a dog walker, camp counselor (teaching folk songs and disco dance), an Avon lady (for about a week), messenger, and librarian. As the Costume Mistress for the Minor Latham Playhouse at Barnard College I washed the costumes and ironed God's robe for the Pageant Plays.

When this piece was written, I was the Co-op Advertising Manager for Crown Publishers and spent most of my days processing contracts for small amounts of money. The rest of the time went to filing, xeroxing, typing, and getting chewed out for my "cavalier attitude" by my boss. After that I went on to be the receptionist and office administrator for a small typesetting company, a job I gave up with great reluctance since I couldn't believe I could live on the money I would make playing music. For many years I would threaten my band with going back, when I had stage fright. "I can always be a receptionist!"

My dream was to be a famous singer and songwriter, so I would take my vacation days and book myself into whatever college and clubs would take a chance on me. I had no records out except for The Fast Folk Musical Magazine, called "The Co-op" in this story. This was an album that came out once a month, headed by Jack Hardy (the Boulevardier with the "lost" hair), and he ran it from the Speakeasy in New York. In those days I was pale and thin and dressed in black with short spiky hair. Now many folk singers look like that, but then they didn't. I enjoyed the freedom of traveling by myself. Here is one of my adventures.

Tuesday November 2, 1982:

I am in bed at the City Line Motel. Exhausted. I traveled eight hours by bus to get here. The ride up was beautiful. I am too tired to think, though, and

zanne vega

at MOJO

november 12, 1982

lume LXII number 7

the interlude

the arts supplement of the lamron

photo by michael batal

am losing the desire and the discipline to write in a journal. Not fair, not fair! I want a record of the days that are going by too quickly, and I desperately need to be more creative. My job is squeezing the spontaneity out of me.

Wednesday

I'm tired. It's lonely here. The motel is far away from anywhere, and there is the constant sound of a car or two passing on the highway outside, the clock ticking, and the rain falling. It has been a gray drizzly day all day.

The tiredness settles over me. A truck goes by. The rain drips and drips in little dances off the awning out front.

This motel is owned by a sad-looking man in the front house—he looks gruff and stern and his mouth turns down, but the ends tip up, just slightly and his eyes are amused.

Mr. H. stopped in there to say hi before we went out for a Coke and pizza, and when I stopped in too, the man said, "This one! This one is so shy! I thought to myself, How can someone so young and shy go traveling all by herself! She doesn't even know where she is!"

I laughed and laughed.

Mr. H. is an interesting man. He seems to think more than some people and seems to be more involved with the students. He's sharp. He's worried about not expanding his mind, about just living here in Watertown for the rest of his life with his wife and young baby. He and his wife are both turning thirty this month, and their baby is a year old.

I was hoping to have lots of time to write, to think, to explore all my feelings out here but I have to get ready for bed. Even though it's only nine-thirty—I have to start now, or I will never get up.

Thursday

Today was another tiring day. I am now at Geneseo, and it feels like one of the longest days of my life.

It's lovely in Watertown. I got up this morning, with no one but the motel man to see me off, and got a taxi to the station. I was early, and as I walked in I saw a guy sitting in one of the chairs. I didn't pay much attention, went and bought my ticket, sat down.

A couple of white-haired ladies came in. They were friends who hadn't seen each other in a while, and they dashed over to talk to each other. They were so sweet!

I felt that I heard each word and impression so clearly; that I was a huge receiver, receiving different stories. They talked in broad Canadian accents, and reminded me of birds, so bright and chirpy, with such skinny sticklike ankles. They talked about their daughters and sons and grandchildren. One woman was going to Ohio for two months, and I thought, This is my mother's country and these ladies are like my grandmother. My mother grew up in a small town in Ohio. I forget that sometimes.

So we all sat around in the station while it rained outside, and the windows fogged.

One little lady said to the other, "We have a new priest in our parish!"

The other one nodded, listening.

"And you should see him! He's young. He's a blond! With his hair all in waves. So bright. He's so cute, it's a wonder he ever made it through the seminary. And he's so holy when he does mass, you'd think he was right in heaven. We are fortunate."

They talked about their husbands.

"Well, he died sixteen years ago now. I was fifty-nine." She shook her head. "It seems like a dream. And the older you get, the more lonesome it is!"

I lost track of the conversations, until somebody said, "He lay there for two months in a coma and then woke up and said, 'Where am I?' He was fine after that. These things are like a miracle!"

Another lady, a third one, listened attentively and nodded. She obviously wanted to join the conversation, but the two friends paid no attention to her, and eventually she stopped listening and nodding, and just looked out the window.

"There's a bus come in," she said loudly, and everyone stood up and began to gather their belongings.

The man who watched me come in said, "Can I help you carry something?"

He reached for my guitar. I gave him a smaller bag to carry. But it was a false alarm, it was the wrong bus, and the ladies all settled down like ruffled birds, preening and patting their hair. I stayed standing up, now that the man had my bag, and stole glances at him when I wasn't watching the ladies.

He had a big silver cross around his neck, on a chain, and his two fingers were yellow from cigarette smoke. I'd never seen anyone with fingers so badly stained, and his eyes were slightly bloodshot, and he fidgeted like something really bothered him. He had wide-set eyes and a moustache, bad skin, and he carried a few duffel bags. I got the feeling he was in some bad trouble or was running away. He looked young. But I didn't say anything to him.

Finally, the right bus came in. It was late, and crowded, and we all piled on. The man with the cross gave me back my bag. I could see where he was sitting, a couple of rows behind me if I turned my head, and I could see his cigarette smoke without turning at all.

I sat by the window and looked out. The sky was a thick gray, and there were bright spots on the trees, still, bright yellow and dark rust against the gray and the green. We went past the dirt rows, and the cows.

Gradually a loud voice from the back drifted its way front, and though I turned my head, I couldn't tell who was speaking. But I saw my Friend with the Cross, two rows back from me, smoking, staring straight ahead and tapping his feet.

The Voice from the Back said: "Do you like to drink? Or do you do weed? The old-fashioned way, huh? I figure what the hell. You do dope, you don't get sick. You know? I like it better. But I drink too. How old are you? How old? Oh, about nineteen or twenty—is that right? Don't be bashful! I wish I were nineteen or twenty. Again! Jesus, those were the days!

"The music was good then. You ramble around, you get high, you listen to music. I was so young. The Beatles just came out! They were on Ed Sullivan. He said, 'We have a really big shew—The Beatles!' And they came out and sang 'I Wanna Hold Your Hand.' And they sang, 'She Was Just Seventeen, If You Know What I Mean.' Ha, ha! Oh, you know what I mean! I was so young. I had a paper route.

"And Dylan! Dylan was cool and he wasn't into religion, not like now. 'Like A Rolling Stone'! Man, that was something! It was so good. And Haight-Ashbury, man, you put a flower in your hair, you get high, you listen to the music. Are you a musician? You look like one. You look like Tom Petty, that's why I thought you were. Oh, man!

"You know, this punk rock, it's okay. At first I didn't like it. I didn't like the name—punk—you know? It sounded sissy to me. But I think it's okay, you know? Not the gags and stuff, but the music. Yeah! Rock and Roll! It Survives!

"Say, you want to get high when we're done here? Oh, no sweat, we're just casual. Don't worry. Just a gesture."

The Voice from the Back continued: "I've been on the road for, oh, three years now. And some weird stuff has happened, you know. The weirdest time I ever had was with two chicks in Texas. You know? Two beautiful women in this truck driving around, blondes, and they picked me up. And I was in there with these two really beautiful chicks! Tanned and in shorts, nice big legs! Man! I thought I had died and gone to heaven! I really did!

"So we had a couple of beers, and then we had a little whiskey. And then we smoked some real good dope, and then she had some crystal under the seat . . ."

Here his voice began to drop and mumble only to rise when he shouted:

"And she had a Dillinger! Man, I don't know what those two chicks were doing with a Dillinger, but I didn't wait to find out! Those crazy chicks! Man, I'm too old to go driving down the highway at ninety miles an hour, getting shot at with bullets and what all! Man, those girls were young, but sure weren't innocent. No, man."

He continued on and on, and his voice blended with the drone of the bus for a while, and I fell asleep. I woke up when the woman reading a romance novel next to me stood up and got off. My Friend with the Cross walked up the aisle to talk to the driver, then came back up, stopped in front of my seat, and said:

"This isn't the express bus."

"That's kind of what I figured," I said. He swung into the seat next to mine.

"Does smoking bother you?" he asked.

"No, go ahead."

"You from Watertown?"

"No, I'm from New York City."

"You going home?"

"Not right away. What about you? Are you from Watertown?" I asked him. He frowned.

"Nope. I wouldn't be from Watertown."

I wondered why.

"I mean, I wouldn't live there. My wife is from there."

"Where are you going?"

"New Orleans. First Tennessee."

"You live there?"

"Mmmhmm." He stretched his legs. The bus started up again.

"So what were you doing in Watertown?" he asked, looking at me sideways.

"I'm a singer. I did a show there yesterday at the college."

"Mmmhmm. You alone?"

"Yes." I pulled my pea coat up to my chin and looked out the window at the leaves and the rain. Behind us two college boys were snickering and talking about the weather.

"This is the kind of day makes you want to kill yourself!" said one. The other one laughed out loud.

"So what were you doing in Watertown?" I asked my companion. He shifted a little in his seat and licked his moustache.

"Time," he said.

"Oh," I said.

An awkward silence grew until he said, "But I'm not no criminal."

"What were you in for?"

He looked uncomfortable, and smiled a little. He spoke so low I could barely hear him.

"Attempted robbery."

It struck us both as funny, and we laughed. I don't know why I was laughing. He had been in six months, and was set free this morning; he was on his way home to his wife, and one-year-old baby daughter, who had won a beauty contest. He was shy about bringing out her pictures, but seemed glad when I wanted to see them.

"See this?" he said, pulling out a little pocketbook with a strap. It was made of some kind of familiar green and white shiny material. I couldn't figure out what it was.

"I made this."

"Oh, yeah? Out of what?"

"Cigarette packets."

I said it was good, and laughed. It seemed fitting.

In Syracuse, we both had an hour to wait. He helped me carry my guitar into the coffee shop. It felt strange to be sitting face to face with him, after sitting beside him all morning. When I left him with my stuff while I went to the bathroom, I wondered if he would rip me off. Attempted robbery. I decided he wouldn't. He wanted to go home.

I came back and my stuff was still there. He was too, awkward and shy and tired. He never smiled, and we both felt tense and strange.

"So what did you do while you were in?"

"Nothing. It was the most boring thing I ever did in my life. I did nothing. I dried out while I was in there. I was an alcoholic." He looked thoughtful. I pointed to his cross.

"Are you Catholic?"

Suddenly his eyes were alert.

"No." He held on to his cross and pulled at it nervously. "But I believe in God," he said firmly. "Do you?"

"I don't know," I said. How could I explain what I believe? What I really believe? I don't know what I really believe. I'd like to believe that each person can control their own destiny, that by doing morning and evening prayers and chanting sincerely you change your life by making good causes, that you should worship Life—life in you, and life bigger than you.

He narrowed his eyes.

"So you believe in yourself, that's what I hear."

"No, it's in yourself, but also outside yourself. It's the whole thing. Life inside and outside you. You're a part of it, and it's bigger than you. Do you know what I mean?"

He smiled and shook his head.

"You believe in yourself, even though you psych yourself out. All I know"—he said, looking at me directly—"is that I've seen miracles happen. And I sure didn't do them. Somebody must have."

He leaned back assuredly. "Somebody must have done it!"

I couldn't really argue with him. I told him my whole family was Buddhist, and it changed our lives, and it was like a miracle. But I didn't want to argue with him. Not on his first day free with him holding on to his cross like that. Maybe I'm a coward. But I changed the subject.

"What did you want to be when you were little?"

He looked embarrassed and thought about it.

"Oh, I don't know. A musician. But I don't have the patience. Oh, I'll bet you really want to be a doctor, right, and you don't have the patience? Have the patients? Get it? My father is a musician in New Orleans. He's a real jokester. But I come from a split home—my parents split up, and my mom, she left, and I grew up with my grandfather, who's a fisherman. I love the water. So I'm going to try to do that when I get back, just start all over again on a boat."

It was nearly time for me to get back on the bus. I gave him two Coop albums with "Cracking" and "Gypsy" on them.

"You're on this?" he said.

"Yeah."

"You're giving this to me?" he said.

"Yeah. If I had time I'd sing them to you. But I have to go."

He seemed troubled.

"Would you really? I have nothing to give you back."

"Oh, don't worry about it. I just want to give this to you."

But he reached in his pocket, and pulled out a medallion, with a picture of Jesus on the front. On the back it said, "I am a Presbyterian." He gave it to me.

"Thanks!" I said. I was sincerely happy.

"I hope these don't get broke," he said. As we walked to the gate, he asked for a pen. I think he wanted me to write on the cover, but there was no time.

"Say! What's your name?"

"Suzanne."

"Suzanne, I'm Dave."

We shook hands.

"Thank you for everything," I said.

"Thank *you*," he said.

"Good luck to you," I said.

"Same to you. Nice meeting you."

We shook hands again, and I turned away and got back on the bus.

Monday

So today I am getting back on the bus for NYC. I wish I had time to write down my impressions of Geneseo and Bloomsburg.

Bloomsburg seems to be a sad little town. I like it. The audience was the best one I've had, I think. They were like me! Reserved, but they liked the music, and came up in between sets and requested songs from the LPs and I thought, "They really came to hear me and not just the 'coffeehouse performer.'"

There's a sadness in this city. Everything smells funny. The mike was dusty and smelled like urine, and the sound system had a huge hum the first set. The hotel smells musty, not all spic and span like Watertown, but the room is big, split-level. Things are chipped, chairs stacked up in the halls.

I get the feeling these students are struggling. Some kids were wearing black, some girls in denim and short hair ...

FIRST DAY OUT

(Age 15)

Here I am at last, I've just jumped off the train
I'm about to start my life as a wanderer in the rain.
I know so many people would give anything to be in
  my shoes
Well, that's all right for them to say, but my shoes are
  soaked right through.

I don't know what made me want to come all the way
  out here
I guess when I was dreaming, my skies were always
  clear.
Now I'm here in a meadow with the rain streaming
  through my hair
I guess this is what you call traveling freely, living with-
  out a care.

Here I am, all by myself, and I'll admit I'm scared
All I've got is my guitar and a couple of dollars to spare
And I know even that's not gonna last me long.

I suppose I could pick myself up and carry myself back
  home
But after what I put my folks through, I think I better
  stay alone.
Anyhow, five years of aching are packed behind this
  plan
Since I was ten, I've wanted to get out of the city and
  live out on the land.

My parents thought I was crazy and I think now maybe
  they're right
But I can still feel the freedom in following the eagle's
  flight.
I just had to come and see what all the songs were
  about
My hope is returning quickly and I don't think there's
  any doubt,

That I'd better start moving if I want to get somewhere
I'll go on to the next town and see what I find there
And stay a while until I go traveling on.

rootless

Were you cut once or twice
too deeply? Do you still bleed, or
Do you finger the scar?
Do you wear this bruise
as a badge upon your breast;
Does it ever let you pass into
underground places?

Or do you only blow
like a wild weed's seed
in whatever wind
will have you?

Are you whole now
mobile
or only
rootless?

night ride

for MG

one small light
two even smaller voices
in one big bus
while the rest of the band is sleeping—

tell me about your uncle.
so he was a soldier?
before we forget you take a beer
and I'll have another.

check on the driver
and keep him awake
he's talking to himself
and it's a good sign—

so tell me about your mother.
is she a pretty woman?
has she ever disappointed you?
does she still love your father?

the rest of the band is breathing
and outside there is a country
that doesn't even realize we are
moving through its darkness

tell me about your sister.
is she older or younger?
was she good or was she mean to you?
does she like her job?

do you hear the clinking
of the bottles left on the seat?
it's good this bus traveling whole
slicing the night with its light.

now why do you look at me strangely,
as though I were very young,
and tell me I must go to sleep,
and dangle your hand from the top bunk,
and lie in the morning and say,
I've never looked more lovely?

tour story

The cats at the Acropolis
are waiting for their meal.
We are on the way to the ferry
in the blinding driving rain.

The bus is doing hairpin turns
across the cliffs.
And we're going to the ferry.
Now we've missed the ferry,

And we're driving back to Athens.
The road is marked by
little wooden houses with crosses on top—
A little wooden shrine to mark each accident.

The sun comes down in shafts
from the sky down to the water.
Until it rains again
and lightning strikes.

Brothers and sisters
I have none
But that man's father
Is my father's son
That man is my son, but Yorky says

It's his Uncle Bert
From Cleckheaton.
And he's driving.

MEN WILL BE MEN

CHORUS
Men will be men and they'll call me the governor
I'll walk through the bar and I'll buy the next round
Because this is my ship and I say it's my destiny
And we'll all go up and go down, we go down, go
   down

Through the town and back up through the avenues
And into the places where people don't stay
Go visit the king and then leave through the window
Go hang with the gang and get lost in the fray

Andy's a saint or a savage, I forget
Depends on the day and if he's eaten yet
He's something to see when he's first out of bed
Not that I'd know, I've just heard it said

Said that, *CHORUS*

Spider's the guy to handle the gun
He'd show me how, but I don't want one
He's oh-so polite for a second-story man
And he's changed his spots as much as anyone can

We know, *CHORUS*

Come and sit with the whores and admire the view
Drink down these beers, I think you've had a few
Yes and don't look at me, I'm not selling today
Over the crowd hear the bartender say

Say that, *CHORUS*

Men will be men and they'll call me the governor
I'll walk through the bar and I'll buy the next round
Because this is my ship and I say it's my destiny
And we'll all go up and go down, we go down, go
   down . . .

AS GIRLS GO

You make a really good girl
As girls go
Still kind of look like a guy
I never thought to wonder why

If I could pull this off
Would I know for certain
The real situation
Behind the curtain

So beautiful
Damsel in distress
Not exactly natural
Stunning nonetheless

What happened to you?
To make you more girl than girls are
Would you ever show or tell?
'Cause you're so good so far

You make a really good girl
As girls go
As girls go
As girls go
As girls go
As girls go

Let's chronicle
The dark side of the life
Did you ever keep the date
With the steel side of the knife?

Doesn't matter to me
Which side of the line
You happen to be
At any given time

You make a really good girl
As girls go
As girls go
As girls go
As girls go
As girls go

naked

**there's something naked
about this man
it's not his clothes
'cause he still has them on**

on being photographed

My English publicist Andy B. told me I was going to have my picture taken by David Bailey. This was exciting news. David Bailey, for those who don't know, is a photographer known for his photos from the sixties, especially of Jean Shrimpton, who he discovered in a sense, and who he also lived with.

He was the prototype for the hero of the Antonioni film *Blow-Up*; the Mod swinging London fashion photographer standing over the Twiggylike model (Verushka, actually) as she sprawls on the floor, while he shoots and shouts, "That's it! Give it to me, baby" and so forth. Of course that was thirty-five years ago, and times have changed. But even so, his legend lingers on—he was married to Catherine Deneuve and lived with Penelope Tree.

So this piece was to be called "The Seven Biggest Women in Rock" or something to that effect, to be published in the August 1997 issue of the UK *Elle* magazine. This is what my English publicist told me. I was skeptical. Biggest women in rock? Who else was doing it? He couldn't remember offhand. Courtney Love? No. Patti Smith? No. Lisa Stansfield was all he could remember. Oh, and by the way they wanted to know would I have my picture taken with Tori Amos? This made me very nervous.

"Tori Amos? Did you see her last album package?" I asked him. "She is suckling a pig at her naked breast. What if she wants to bring a pig to the session?"

"There will be no pigs at the session," Andy reassures me.

"Yes, but how do you know? What if this is a concept she wants to develop? I don't think this is such a good idea. I just had a baby, well, two years ago, and I want them to think about my lighting and stuff." I am fretting. "Not that I am any kind of diva or anything, that's not me at all."

"Not at all," my publicist agrees diplomatically. "I'll talk to them and we'll see what we can do."

The morning arrives. What am I going to wear? "It's supposed to be natural," says Andy. "Just wear something cool, there'll be no stylists or anything, they want you looking natural." Oh, I think to myself, natural; well, I'll wear black leather, then, since that's what I wear on the road anyway, but I think I should come wearing my false eyelashes though, since my features are pale and plain on their own.

I stare at my face in the hotel mirror. Will my face behave today? I never can tell what persona will come leaping out. My brother used to say I had a face like a Victorian spinster, which I didn't like, but thought was accurate. I peer over at my two-year-old daughter Ruby, who is happily playing with her plastic animals. She takes them with her on the road in a box. This morning many of them are lying bellies up on the hotel room floor, while she tenderly kisses each one's animated little face. She is not thinking about her face and whether it will behave; she is at that age where she is enchanted by her reflection and rightly so.

After I see that she is happy, I glue half a strand of false eyelashes to my upper lids, kiss my husband good-bye, and sail out of the hotel, figuring there will be someone there at the shoot at least to do makeup, and they can finish the job I have so haphazardly begun. The effect right now is a little strange, I will admit—no lipstick or mascara; just these bits of hair hanging off my upper lids. But I like the effect when all the makeup is done—feline and exotic—and I don't know that the makeup girl will have them with her, especially so early in the morning, so I slap sunglasses on my face and hope for the best.

Andy is in a cheery mood. "Oh, the leather is perfect!" he breathes, as I jump into his car. What I'm wearing is what he's wearing; black leather jacket, T-shirt, sunglasses, black denim pants, boots. The music business uniform.

"Oh, thanks," I say, attempting nonchalance. I have brought a couple of other jackets in case it's not quite perfect, or in case David Bailey wants me to roll around on the floor while he stands over me, shouting.

"By the way, it's no longer 'The Seven Biggest Women In Rock.' It's been expanded to eighteen," he says, drawing on a cigarette, and screeching around the corner in the car.

"'The Eighteen Biggest Women in Rock'? That sounds bizarre," I say. "Sounds like it depends on who is in town." It's ten in the morning, which feels to my jet-lagged brain like the crack of dawn, but here we are pulling up to a cobblestoned side street. We rap on the door; we are met at the door by an assistant and brought up to the second story to meet the man himself.

Tori Amos is the first one here. Oh, no! I am dismayed. There she is, engrossed in conversation with David Bailey. He looks a bit rotund, with bright twinkly eyes. He looks over and winks at me. I look at Andy in help-less panic.

"I thought we were having our pictures taken separately?" I hiss.

"You are," he says.

"I thought I was first because of this show in Derby I have to do later today?"

"You are!" he says under his breath, squinting and exhaling his cigarette.

Tori turns to me, and extends her hand. "Hi, Suzanne, it's so nice to meet you," she says. I stop hissing, and straighten up and behave myself.

"Oh, very nice to meet you too, I've read so much about you," I say.

"Is it true you just had a baby?" she asks.

"Well, yes—a couple of years ago, anyway," I say.

We continue talking, and she suddenly reveals to me a tragedy she had experienced recently, which takes me aback with its intimacy. She is forth-right, and sincere, and mesmerizing, and I find myself drawn into her pri-vate world almost against my will. Unconsciously I notice her skin is more olive than in her photos, where she is chalk white; her cheekbones and mouth are so prominent she appears almost American Indian. She has an otherworldly, almost elfin presence.

Her stylist comes in, a black woman from somewhere—they embrace like long-lost friends. Apparently there is a rack of clothes upstairs for her to examine. What!? I am jealous. But there is no time for that, because here's David Bailey who wants to look at me for a minute. Andy has shoved a cup of tea with milk and sugar into my hands, the first of many.

I find myself looking into a roguish face with mischievous eyes that stare at me a long while. I find myself turning red. What's he thinking? Is he thinking, oh, she's a cool classic beauty like my ex-wife Catherine Deneuve?

"You've a bit of Penelope Tree about you," he rasps out, finally. Oh. It's the waif persona leaping out of my face when I least expect it. Penelope Tree was a famous model from the sixties, and to me she always looked a bit freakish and spidery with huge eyes and long skinny limbs, but really I shouldn't complain—she was an icon of sorts and they did live together. I am beginning to obsess about the stupid eyelashes and wonder if they are too much. But I am turning red again as he is staring into my face in a way that makes me feel peeled of all skin, as if he finds what's underneath to be terribly amusing.

We discuss Penelope Tree and her thyroid condition for a while until he says, "Are you all right? You're not quite all here today, are you?" He twinkles severely, if such a thing is possible.

"No, I'm fine. I'm just nervous. I hate having my picture taken." And I do. The thought of being judged for life by what happens to be on the outside of my head is absurd to me.

"Oh, no need to be nervous," he says, giving my hand a squeeze, as though he delights in my being nervous, and as though we are sharing a wicked secret. Does he share this wicked secret with Tori Amos too? "Come and meet the girl who'll do your makeup," he says and hands me over to a feline and exotic girl. She looks the way I'm trying to look!

Her cool appraising eye notes the bits of false eyelashes and the lack of any other makeup, and she says tactfully, "Is this the way you would like to be photographed? Or would you like a little more?"

I explain that I had hoped she would do more, of course, I had only glued these on in case she didn't have any herself. She is a girl from the American Midwest, near Chicago, so we chat about techniques of makeup application, and about America.

"I couldn't take Chicago. The weather drove me out of my head," she said.

"And how long have you been here?" I ask.

"About a year. But I didn't like it at first. I think I was just lonely. It can drive you out of your head." She says this while plastering my face with foundation. I think about being "driven out of one's head" until—

"Remember it's black and white!" shouts David Bailey from across the loft. I suggest a thin black line over my upper eyelid, and a well-defined mouth with some pink frosted lipstick, which will bleach out the tension around my mouth, and any bags under my eyes, when he adjusts the white level in the camera. She takes these suggestions well, with a good sense of humor in her almond-shaped eyes, and then we stop for another tea break before she does my lips.

My own eyes begin to focus on some photographs against the painted white brick walls across his loft. I can't quite make out what they are. Abstractions? Close-up black-and-white pictures of some organic substance, like a plant? Oh, it's a large uncircumcised penis in repose. And the owner of this penis has black skin, so it gleams with a dark luster in this print. Oh, and here's a vagina under close scrutiny as well, complete with hair; and here is a painting showing a woman from the same angle. Maybe this explains the charged atmosphere in the air; the faintly combative yet festive feeling of sexual challenge in the room that comes from looking and being looked at.

I turn around to have my face completed, when I see Kate Spicer, the journalist for the piece, furtively trying to catch my eye so she can ask me a few questions. She sidles up to me and begins to talk in a voice barely above a whisper.

"So, um," she says, juggling a cup of tea with a tape recorder and a notebook in her lap, "do you mind my asking you some things?"

"No, sure, go right ahead," I say, while the makeup girl takes the lipstick brush out of my mouth, where it has fallen in by accident.

"Do you feel you write from a particularly female point of view?" she says.

"No, no, I don't. The songs are very often from a neutral point of view, like 'Small Blue Thing,' or masculine like 'Tom's Diner,' or 'Luka,' or 'Rock in This Pocket.'"

"Oh. I see," she says, looking down to see if her tape recorder is going. I wonder if I have just shot down the premise for her Women in Music piece. I hurry on.

"I mean, obviously a song like 'Birth-day' is written from a feminine perspective, because it's about giving birth. Not just physically—I thought that would be sort of repulsive—but spiritually as well. Some people can't figure it out and assume it's about a drug experience."

She looks up and laughs. "Really?"

"Yes, or about violent sex. Well, giving birth can be a drug experience, depending on how it goes for you. Mine certainly was."

She opens her mouth to ask another question when we are interrupted by a rude bark from across the room. It's David Bailey shouting.

"You journalist! Stop bothering her! She's having her makeup done! You know what I think of you! You're lower than the chewing gum on the doorstep, you are! Honestly! I'll throw you right out of here!"

He scowls and delivers this in a high-pitched sharp voice that hits like little pebbles; she winces, smiles apologetically, and scurries off to sit with Tori Amos. But wait! I am thinking. We were just getting started! As I watch (and as the makeup girl puts on the final outline of my mouth, while talking to me about her English boyfriend), Tori is mesmerizing the journalist. They are having a long intimate chat in low tones. Tori's hand is on the journalist's knee. What are they talking about? I'll never know because—

Finally my face is done. The powder is dusted on, and it's time to be marched off in front of the lens, time for the moment of truth. I look for the lights. I don't see any. He's using natural daylight; I prefer a white hot artificial light three inches from my face which erases everything on it. He has an assistant who scurries around, doing his bidding, opening the shutters, changing the backdrop, raising the silver hoop that they use to fill in the light. David Bailey stares at me and smiles. Suddenly I feel like screaming with giggles.

"How are you doing, kid?" he says.

"Okay," I say. Out of the corner of my eye I see a beautiful woman in a dress mopping the floor; her brightly clothed and graceful rear end is protruding out of the doorway of the studio next door. David is used to this sight, I guess, because he continues to stare at my face, scowling and smiling bemusedly at the same time.

Some photographers want you to move. They'll ask you to turn this way or that way, touch yourself (meaning your face and neck, sometimes your body as well), move your hands, relax your mouth, lift your chin, lower your head, smile, look at the camera. I have had photographers shout, "With all the warmth you have within you, will you please look at this camera!" I have been dragged through neighborhoods in New York City with my eyes swelling and tearing from the sun, and I still hear, "Miss Vega, we insist that you cooperate with us. Please look at this camera with just a hint of a smile, if you will!" Which doesn't make anyone feel like smiling.

But David doesn't want me to move at all. He doesn't want me to roll on the floor while he towers over me. He doesn't want me leaping spontaneously in the air. He wants me perfectly still.

"Hold it! That's it. Don't move," he glowers at me. "It's a slow exposure."

I try not to move. "You moved!" he shouts.

"Did not," I mumble. "We call it breathing on my planet."

"What?"

"Nothing."

"And make your eyes wider. Open your eyes. They were bigger before."

How could they possibly have been bigger before?

"They were not bigger before."

"They were. Now don't move."

I am reminded of a session I did for my other brother who is also a photographer. He was trying some new technique that consisted of my sitting on the couch while he held the camera into my face, and I was not to move for two minutes or so. I was seized then with uncontrollable itching, and it enraged him—I still have memories of him screaming at me, "You moved!"

But now, David Bailey is still peering and muttering instructions to his assistant. For a minute I can see the reflection of my eye in the lens. Perhaps if I can keep this reflection, I can have some control! I can be like my daughter, two years old and peering happily into the mirror. But I must be looking pensive, because he suddenly whispers while staring fiercely into my eyes, "Glimmer of hope, darling."

This strikes me as poetic and funny. I shriek with laughter, which annoys him. I like that! Not the "darling" part, but the other part. But he doesn't want me laughing. So I think about a soft cloudy day with a glimmer of sun somewhere in the sky. What he wants is a little smile, and I know that. So I try to oblige him.

I am getting weary, I have to admit. The sun is in my eyes. I'm sleepy. There is nothing to look at but his grizzled face. I sigh. I tap my feet. I try and listen to the music. What is the music? Billie Holiday? He can feel that he's losing my attention. "Do you want more tea?" he says, followed by, "So you had a baby recently?"

"Well, yes, two years ago," I say, snapping to attention. He tells me of his own two young children, and confides to me that he's been living his life backward. I am drawn in again! We are conspirators with a wicked secret once more.

"Don't move! That's fine, that's lovely," he shouts, and I freeze and try to keep my face looking lively, and lovely. I try and think of something glamorous, like Catherine Deneuve. I try to think of anything I can, but nothing sticks. All I can do is stare at the camera with no clue of what I am projecting, what I look like, what he sees, what he wants, or what the camera sees. I hope that as a graphic image it's interesting at the very least. All I can do is look at the camera, which doesn't "see" anything. All it can do is register—shapes, shades of color, tones of black and white, and lines.

Much has been written about the phenomenon of picture-taking, and how some tribes fear that if you take their picture, you steal their soul.

Matthew Modine, the actor, met a fan who wanted his picture to prove she had really met him. He agreed, and afterward when she was done he looked at me and said, "They TAKE your picture," snatching the air in front of my face. I was sympathetic. In the case of Princess Diana, it was certainly true; the legend will always be that her life and soul were taken by the paparazzi, as well as her photograph, no matter what the verdict in court ends up to be.

But that is in the future, and I am here voluntarily, not just to have my picture "taken," but to "give" my picture, so to speak. Have I failed by not being able to project something lively and emotional in front of a piece of machinery? I won't know till the piece comes out. But, it seems the shoot is over. We are both relieved. So is the assistant. David Bailey is beaming at me and we walk back to the group holding hands and smiling. I am dizzy, as though I have eaten too much sugar. Come to think of it, after four cups of tea, my insides are floating in caffeine and sugar.

But that's what the scene is like; a sugar rush. Sandie Shaw has arrived and is having her makeup done. "Oh, hello," she says. "I always wanted to meet you." Why? I wonder. "I heard you are a Buddhist, and so am I," she says, and we talk about the fact that I used to practice, and about other things. Her eyes are grave; she says, "It's hard to be sincere in an atmosphere like this," and I suppose I know what she means.

But because the tension of "performing" is over, I am in a strange new mood; I have the giddy sense that we are all wonderful new friends; we have shared intimacies; we have looked at one another and been looked at; we are all so vulnerable here; everybody looks so terrific! It's fake, the way energy from sugar is, but very nice while it lasts.

I kiss everyone good-bye, and I feel as though we will all continue meeting like this now for years to come. It's an illusion, of course. But I wish Tori Amos the best, as they set up for her shoot. Everyone is being shot separately, it seems. The makeup girl promises me free cosmetics. I am happy. I kiss David Bailey good-bye, and he winks and squeezes my hand. Andy and I bound out into the sunshine to catch a train, so I can make the show later that day.

"He's funny, isn't he?" said Andy. "He kept winking at me."

On the way to the train he fills me in on more gossip—one girl got dropped from this piece and from her record label on the same day. I had never heard of her.

It's not till I arrive in Derby that I realize I have left everything behind at that shoot—performing jacket, passport, wallet, keys, money. Andy B. is an angel, and arranges to have them sent by train that night, but I feel ashamed. I was duped by the atmosphere there! I forgot my priorities! Unconsciously I wanted to stay all day, obviously, and put on costumes and play in front of the camera, smiling into the mirror at my reflection and feeling pleased.

Well, in a month or so, the piece comes out. It's called "Girl Power," though on the cover it reads "Rock Divas by David Bailey." There's a huge picture of k. d. lang, looking manly. A huge picture of Lisa Stansfield, looking blowsy and hurt, wreathed in cigarette smoke. Some women I had never heard of. A small picture of a calm Sandie Shaw, saying, "I invented divas. Only the true things with integrity stick around." The picture of Tori Amos is last—she looks ethereal, like a fairy with a tiara of flowers, dressed in tulle. Her expression is not as poised as I've seen her in the past, as she has a "you-have-to-be-kidding-me" look in her eyes, which I can't recall seeing before in any of her photographs.

But the perfect picture belongs to Justine Frischmann, from the band Elastica. Her hands are in her pockets, pulling the waistband of her trousers down, showing an inch of underwear; her body is arched back in an insouciant arc; her black-T-shirted breasts are neatly aimed up to the top of the page; her eyes show humor in a tough squint; her full lips are a cross between a smile and a sneer. She has no jewelry, and very little make-up. Graphically, it's beautiful, a strong slash across the page. Emotionally, it's perfect as well—with the right side of her face she is laughing, with the left she is snarling.

Mine? Well, it's not very rock-n-roll. Mine is near the end; I share the page with Cerys Mathews. Compared to the others, I am stark upright, alabaster, and virginal looking. The focus is on my eyes, which are very wide, as you might imagine, considering; the other focus seems to be on my jaw, which is forbidding. How can a jawbone look virginal? But it does. The picture says, "You can take my picture, you can look at me. But I am looking at you, as well. You are not taking anything I don't want you to have. You can take my face, but you may not have what's behind it." There's a slight bit of humor, but not much. Mostly I look maidenly, untouchable, aloof, and emotionally detached. Which, strangely enough, is what I've been told I'm like by the media all these years. It is pretty enough, but not what I meant to look like. Nor is it what I feel like.

I compare it with a self-portrait I drew many years ago. I do not draw often, so it's not technically good—it's exaggerated, distorted and elongated. There is no humor in this drawing. But you can clearly see it is the same person, though the self-portrait looks more disturbed, with colder eyes and a pursed mouth.

I understand why younger female artists coming up now not only write their own lyrics and play their own instruments, but manufacture their own images, having a photographer on their team that they work with exclusively. I am thinking of P. J. Harvey, whose first and second albums were promoted in the press with a slew of intimate photographs; some hideously deformed, with her face and lips pressed against a pane of glass, some with her being naked, swinging her hair around in a wide wet circle.

Why would she want to look like that, as opposed to say, Audrey Hepburn? Because she doesn't want to be judged from the outside; she wants to be looked at from the inside out. Why would Sinead O'Connor shave her head? Same reason. She felt it made her look beautiful, and it gives her photos a figurative quality that is unmistakable—she looks like a nun or a prisoner, something outside the mainstream, something unfathomable.

After the shoot is done, I find a few pictures of David Bailey, funnily enough. There he is in the newspaper, with his grizzled seaman's face and pouchy eyes peering at me in black and white. Here he is again, straddling his wife on a bed—she has a low-cut dress on and is upside down in full makeup—he is looking down at her bosom.

Then, in the back of a book I keep in the bedroom, called *The Sixties: A Decade in Vogue,* I see the image I first associated with him; but it seems I had it wrong. He is rolling around on the floor, while the model is towering over him. He is shooting up at her, clawing at her with his hand, while she is poised and appears to be in perfect control. Now that would be more like it.

plain

I've been plain.
I wear this plainness proudly.
It was my badge
In everyday life.

I am nothing more
Than grain in the wood
And rust on steel.
A town you went through once
Then forgot.
A girl on a step.

I had a moment of beauty.

Plain is the mask
that lets me
Into the places
Where people are working.

So don't glitter
In front of me.
I'll turn from you
And choose what I know.

BOOK & A COVER

What's that they told you
about a book & a cover?
Don't judge so quickly,
Is it too much to remember?
'Cause pictures lie,
you know.
I'll show
it's so.
Just give it one thought.

What's that they taught you?
To revere a kind of beauty?
To paint on that pretty veneer
and try to hide whatever's dirty?
Well, faces lie.
You'll see
no sympathy.
Just give it one thought.

Come here and I will whisper true
about the things I know of you,
and you will recognize them,
always . . .

As near to you as breath and bone,
so dear to me, and yours alone,
and I will love you for them,
always . . .

What's that they tell you
about a book & a cover?
Don't judge so quickly.
They'll tell you one thing and then another.
But see what lies
within,
under the skin.
Just give it one thought.

modesty

Japanese girl
Her collar so high
Her pencil so quick
Her smile is shy
Her hands are small
And brown.

The way she's covered up
Makes me want
One small unfolding
And the chance
To caress.

STOCKINGS

I don't care for tights, she says
and does not tell me why
She hikes her skirt above her knee
revealing one brown thigh

I see, I say, and wonder at
her slender little fingers
How cleverly they pull upon
the threads of recent slumbers

Do you know where friendship ends
and passion does begin?
It's between the binding of
her stockings and her skin.
(oh yeah)

She stayed up so late I thought
she'd ask me to go dance
But something in the way she laughed
told me I had no chance

The fiction in her family
was that she was never nice
I'd say she was very
I just did not see the price

Do you know where friendship ends
and passion does begin?
When the gin and tonic
makes the room begin to spin.
(oh yeah)

There may be attraction here
but it will never flower
So I'm assigned to read her mind, now
in this witching hour

Here's no game for those who claim
to be easily bruised
But how can I complain
when she's so easily amused?

Do you know where friendship ends
and passion does begin?
(When she does not show you
the way out on the way in)—
It's between the binding
of her stockings and her skin.
(oh yeah)

on MASCULINITY

(*Esquire* magazine, October 1991)

One of my earliest memories is as follows: I am sitting with my first boyfriend. His name is Markie and he is my next-door neighbor. We are both four years old. I look over at him and say, When I grow up, I am going to marry you. He looks back at me and says, When I grow up, I am going to be a fireman and squirt water all over you. I thought his comment was only mildly amusing, but I recall that my parents found it really funny. I suppose he was expressing a traditionally masculine sentiment, the phallic implications of which were not lost on them.

This phase of going around wanting to marry people was short-lived. By the age of eleven, I had decided that getting married was for wimps. So was being feminine, for that matter. I no longer wanted to marry a man. I wanted to join the ranks of men. So I cut my long blond hair into a bowl shape around my head, wore work boots and blue jeans and a pea coat. I began to think of myself as a psychic soldier, one who would resist and endure: honest, straightforward, courageous. I didn't play with makeup. I studied karate. In my basement there was a bucket of sand and gravel in case of fire. When I did my laundry down there, I would sit on the windowsill in the dark and grind my knuckles into the gravel until specks of blood appeared. I wanted my hands to be hard and callused. I wanted to be manly.

Around this time I was impressed by yet another image. My sixth-grade teacher built a pyramid out of wheels and sticks, objects that were frail in themselves, but when he put the pyramid on the floor and leaned on it, it maintained its shape. Beautifully and gracefully it resisted the pressure of his weight, and I decided that henceforth I wanted to be like the pyramid, which was neither masculine nor feminine; it was abstract.

But even abstract shapes can't escape the fate of being assigned one sex or the other. Traditionally, protrusions, weapons, buildings, mountains are masculine. And recessions, bowls, valleys, oceans are seen as feminine. Of course, this is silly.

A woman is as capable of protruding as a man is (she can have a loud personality, or big breasts with pointed cones on them, for example). A man can be as yielding, as receptive, as any woman.

I was asked once in an interview: Who impersonates sex for me? I tried to explain that I prefer to handle these things myself, but I did suppose I could send my sister as an impersonator if I wasn't up to it. The interviewer nodded politely and repeated the question. He meant, of course, who do I find sexy? Who personified sex for me? I think people are sexy when they have a sense of humor, when they are smart, when they have some sense of style, when they are kind, when they express their own opinions, when they are creative, when they have character. These are not particularly masculine traits. I prefer to believe that in our hearts and minds, we are more similar than not. And my answer to the interview question was,

My boyfriend A. and Marlene Dietrich.

MARLENE ON THE WALL

Even if I am in love with you
All this to say, what's it to you?
Observe the blood, the rose tattoo
Of the fingerprints on me from you

Other evidence has shown
That you and I are still alone
We skirt around the danger zone
And don't talk about it later

Marlene watches from the wall
Her mocking smile says it all
As she records the rise and fall
Of every soldier passing

But the only soldier now is me
I'm fighting things I cannot see
I think it's called my destiny
That I am changing

Marlene on the wall

I walk to your house in the afternoon
By the butcher shop with the sawdust strewn
"Don't give away the goods too soon"
Is what she might have told me

And I tried so hard to resist
When you held me in your handsome fist
And reminded me of the night we kissed
And of why I should be leaving . . .

Marlene watches from the wall
Her mocking smile says it all
As she records the rise and fall
Of every man who's been here

But the only one here now is me
I'm fighting things I cannot see
I think it's called my destiny
That I am changing

Marlene on the wall

HEADSHOTS

The sign said "Headshots"
And that was all,
A picture of a boy
And a number you could call,
Two eyes in the shade
A mouth so sad and small,
It's strange the way a shadow
Can fall across the wall,
And make the difference
In what you see
Ah . . .

He's just a poster, but
He's everywhere,
A face under a street lamp
Ripped and hanging in the air,
Turn the corner
And he's still there,
Watching all the people
Who are passing unaware,
Is there a judgment
In what he sees?
Ah . . .

On a day
As cold
And gray
As today . . .

The sign says "Headshots"
It's all I see,
A boy becomes a picture
Of guilt and sympathy,
And so I think of you
In memory
Of the days we were together,
And I knew that you loved me
That was the difference
In what we see,
But that's history . . .
Ah . . .

(IF YOU WERE)
IN MY MOVIE

If you were in my movie
I'd have you as the doctor
Small black bag
And a big black coat

I'd have you make a
  house call
To the woman
You could lay your
Diagnostic hand
Upon her belly and her
  throat

If you were in my movie
You could be the detective
You could sit behind the
  desk
With a question on your lip

Examine her for motive
Investigate the scene
In the ever-present danger
Keep the holster at your hip

If you were in my movie
If you were in my movie
If you were in my movie

If you were in my movie
You could be the priest
Long black frock
White collar at the neck

You could come to the con-
  fession
You could give a girl a thrill
You could save her from
  her passion
Keep her body in check

If you were in my movie
If you were in my movie
If you were in my movie

If you were in my movie
You could be the gangster
Double-breasted pin-striped
Man with the cigarette

Go running down the alley
With a double-crossing
  blonde
Explaining to the jury
That you hadn't done any-
  thing yet

If you were in my movie . . .

to c l

I like the boys
all dressed in black
The bashful ones
In the pointed shoes
The skinny ones
In the tight black clothes
The ones on fire
With the inner desire
And a flame in their eyes.
The ones from the city
The ones who spend time in their rooms
Writing in their notebooks
Going to film school
Coming out at night
To the clubs.
Dangerously clever
And sweetly shy.

I only turned to see
What hand had set this inner field alight
Against the flame I see
The outline of a man against a night

Take back your sympathy
I do not need to drink that bitter stuff
I'd rather break the thread
That bound us close, and say we called a bluff

A casual match
In a very dry field
What could be
The season's yield?

My eyes have gone to coal
It's nothing I would be concerned about
Observe the moment
When the heat of love becomes the chill of doubt

A casual match
In a very dry field
Fire and ash
Is the season's yield

We look for a sign
But it is not revealed
Fire and ash is the
Season's yield

LIGHTNING

(Taken from *Songs from Liquid Days* by **Philip Glass**)

Lightning struck a while ago
And it's blazing much too fast
But give it rain of waiting time
And it will surely pass
Blow over

And it's happening so quickly
As I feel the flaming time
And I grope about the embers
To relieve my stormy mind
Blow over

Shaken this has left me
And laughing and undone
With a blinding bolt of sleeplessness
That's just begun

And a windy crazy running
Through the nights and through the days
And a crackling
Of the time burned away
Burned away

Now I feel it in my blood
All hot and sharp and white
With a whipcrack and a thunder
And a flash of flooding light

But there'll be a thick and smoky
Silence in the air
When the fire finally dies
And I'm wondering who'll be left there

In the ashes of the time
Burned away
Burned away

FREEZE TAG

We go to the playground
In the wintertime
The sun is fading fast
Upon the slides into the
    past
Upon the swings of indeci-
    sion
In the wintertime

In the dimming diamonds
Scattering in the park
In the tickling
And the trembling
Of freeze tag
In the dark

We play that we're actors
On a movie screen
I will be Dietrich
And you can be Dean

You stand
With your hand
In your pocket
And lean against the wall
You will be Bogart
And I will be
Bacall

And we can only say yes
    now
To the sky, to the street, to
    the night

Slow fade now to black
Play me one more game
Of chivalry
You and me
Do you see
Where I've been hiding
In this hide-and-seek?

We go to the playground
In the wintertime
The sun is fading fast
Upon the slides into the
    past
Upon the swings of indeci-
    sion
In the wintertime
Wintertime
Wintertime

We can only say yes now
To the sky, to the street, to
    the night
We can only say yes now
To the sky, to the street, to
    the night

PLAYING

(Age 15)

Here I am and there I go
I'm flying high and running low
I'll wait for you if you want me to
but I'll be damned if I'll stop the show

You can play if you want to
but you have to know how to run
The game you see is get up early enough
to catch the sun

Let's go there's no time to lose
no time to pick no time to choose
When you hear the call just gather it all
we'll see how long you keep the blues

You can play if you want to
but you have to know how to win
If you fall don't take it hard
just get back up again

And make your mind up quickly
'cause the game is going fast
and the race is to the swift
and I'm not planning to be last

Honey don't take so long to decide
I mean you can't even tell me that you've tried
Jump right in and don't you know
that the time is now and you can't be slow
Are you going to stand and watch along the side?

See me go I'm not earthbound
I barely touch upon the ground
Like Mercury I'm sailing free
maybe I'll catch you next time around

You can play if you want to
but you have to know how to live
I can teach you how to play
but I can't teach you how to live

NO CHEAP THRILL

Ante up. And don't be shy.
Who is that man who is catching my eye?
What's underneath all of the deadpan face?
Sitting so pretty with a criminal grace?

Lamebrain Pete wants to Spit in the Sea.
He's got a cool hand but it isn't for me.
Butcher Boy thinks he'll be splitting the pot.
But I've seen what he's got and it isn't a lot.

(When deuces are wild you can follow the queen.
I'd go too except I know where she's been.)

I'll see you, I'll call you, I'll raise you
But it's no cheap thrill
It will cost you, cost you, cost you
Anything you have to pay.

I limit the straddles, and you shuffle and deal.
When will the dealer reveal how he feels?
Is the lucky beginner just a five-card stud?
Is this winning streak going to be nipped in the bud?

I'll see you, I'll call you, I'll raise you
But it's no cheap thrill
It will cost you, cost you, cost you
Anything you have to pay.

I'll match you, I'll bet you, I'll play you,
But it's no cheap thrill
It will cost you, cost you, cost you
Anything you have to pay.

rough you up

Let me
Rough you up
I'm not new
Neither are you

Let me
Make my mark
Stain and rumple
Crush and crumple

I know you
And you can take it.

shame

A hundred birds rose up
The day I came to see you
They circled in the air
And landed on the ice.

It was very early morning
The train pulled from the station
It sang softly to itself
Don't worry, I'll be there soon.

Through a town in the midwest
with buildings of brick and steel
From the 1930s, near the
Factory part of town, advertising
Baking soda, coffee;
Everything looked forward to the place
  that we would meet.

The day I left you,
The train pulled from the station.
The sky was blank and blue.
With no birds. Not one.

concubine

Here in the dirty apartment
Naked like a concubine
Wrapped in an old yellow blanket
That is yours and this was mine

Here in the ashes
and the matches and the glasses
and the cigarettes, the magazines,
the crackers and the crumbs

drunken tune

Oh, shut up.
I'm drunk now, and mean.
The memories are poison.
They eat at my brain.
The dreams don't help either.

Some woman with a whore's face
Was rude at the restaurant
Now my heart is aggravated
And I want to fight.

She hit me with the brush
that sweeps the crumbs.
Then she asked us to leave with no reason.

I won't calm down.
Or be quiet either.
You be quiet yourself.
I'll do what I like.

I'm cutting my hair
In bangs to spite my face.
And spite you too, so there.
So there, so there.

I'll walk down this alley
And the cobblestones twist my ankles
And I don't care
And I'll shout at you if I want.

Yes, well. On this weekend
That child would be
Eleven years old now?
Or ten. I won a round
of drinks at the bar on the strip,
from one to two A.M.,
for the hour we lost, and the child we lost,
and I lost the drinks, too, on the way home.
Really bad, but that was life back then, and
I'm married now, and it's different.

But I'm still drunk and I'm angry
and my heart is sore
in this foreign city.

OUT OF REACH

for RM

I am looking through your eyes again
at the maze there in your head
I heard what you just said
and I believe your mind is bending

I have followed you as long as I could
and once or twice I even thought I understood
and now I'm standing here alone
while you fly right out of reach
telling me your broken drunken speech
there was written by my hand.

All you're asking for is a simple human touch
Is that so very much? well that depends on where you
    want it

You don't know about the times I have wished the sky
    would just give up
and let the stars come falling crashing spinning down
and never stop
and now you say you hear the voice of reason
laugh right at you
maybe it's true.
maybe it ought to.

Now you want to know
if I can fix your bleeding face
if I can bring you back some grace
if I have seen your honor somewhere

if I could take you in my arms and make you whole
if I could break the spell and make you well
I would have done it long ago
If I could hold you all together
if I had the magic power
If I had the healing touch
maybe I could make you know how much
I have needed you.

Somewhere
in a city
far away from us now
is a side street
with a small store
with books, about music.

When we enter
we are laughing.
we have just
walked through the market place
with the singing
and the selling,
in a dusty afternoon
of fish and fruit and sweaters
and I'm longing
for something   side street
I think it's a drink.

Instead we enter
the small side street
with the bookstore
and we're laughing
everyone turns as we step in—it's
an older man with a woman
who has paid and is leaving.

We're suddenly silent
our feet upon the carpet.
The old man's store
is like a library
and here I find
a strange
book
which I had been
thirsting for.

NIGHT SONG

(Age 15)

It's two o'clock this morning
every sane person is asleep
I wonder where you are tonight
and down whose hallways do you creep
I know you, you're out somewhere
you know you shouldn't be
Anyhow, wherever you are, I know you're not thinking
of me.

So it's good night
Maybe I'll see you in the morning
Soldier of the night
You try to combat the new day dawning
Do you fear the light?
Or do you fear the emptiness in you yawning?

So you search for life by night
Hidden from sight
Safe within the night
Lost in your crazy flight
And looking for the fight
That may prove you are someone
But you can't stop the rising sun.

When the sun comes up, the world can see your face
You slink along the sidewalk, outnumbered and out of
place
All your boldness is gone, you stand there tongue-tied
and shy

And then it's good night
You put on your criminal disguise
Make sure your mask is tight
Safe now from all accusing eyes
You let loose in delight
Attacking night walkers by surprise
Protected by the night
You feel you have the right
To destroy all in your way
With the anger built by day
Now you have learned to kill
And you do it just for spite
The twisted rules of night
Have caught you in its game
Nobody knows your name
But the day will come
And you'll have no place to run

Because you can't stop the rising sun.

If you want me
You can find me
Left of center
Off of the strip
In the outskirts
In the fringes
In the corner
Out of the grip

When they ask me
"What are you looking at?"
I always answer
"Nothing much" (not much)
I think they know that
I'm looking at them
I think they think
I must be out of touch

But I'm only
In the outskirts
In the fringes
On the edge
And off the avenue
If you want me
You can find me
Left of center
Wondering about you

I think that somehow
Somewhere inside of us
We must be similar
If not the same
So I continue
To be wanting you
Left of center
Against the grain

LEFT OF

If you want me
You can find me
Left of center
Off of the strip
In the outskirts
In the fringes
In the corner
Out of the grip

When they ask me
"What are you looking at?"
I always answer
"Nothing much" (not much)
I think they know that
I'm looking at them
I think they think
I must be out of touch

But I'm only
In the outskirts
And in the fringes
On the edge
And off the avenue
And if you want me
You can find me
Left of center
Wondering about you
Wondering about you

CENTER

SOME JOURNEY

If I had met you on some journey
Where would we be now?
If we had met on some eastbound train
Through some black sleeping town

Would you have worn your silken robes
All made of royal blue?
Would I have dressed in smoke and fire
For you to see through?

If we had met in a darkened room
Where people do not stay
But shadows touch and pass right through
And never see the day

Would you have taken me upstairs
And turned the lamplight low?
Would I have shown my secret self
And disappeared like the snow?

Oh, I could have played your little girl
Or I could have played your wife
I could have played your mistress
Running danger down through your life

I could have played your lady fair
All dressed in lace like the foam from the sea
I could have been your woman of the road
As long as you did not come back home to me

But as it is, we live in the city
And everything stays in place
Instead we meet on the open sidewalk
And it's well I know your face

We talk and talk, we tell the truth
There are no shadows here
But when I look into your eyes
I wonder what might have been here

Because if I had met you on some journey
Where would we be now?

BLACK

I am at your halfway station, darling, and I've been
waiting for your train.
I am at your halfway station, darling, and I've been
waiting for your train.
But you've been too long, darling, and it looks like rain.

I have seen these strange little girls who come up to you
and they don't know when to stop.
I have watched your eye as it follows the line of the leg
right up to the top.
Now Betty Sue and Mary Jane have come around to
play again,
but I am standing at your door and I do believe I'll tell
them to go home.

There's this black widow spider, darling, and she's been
walking on my hand.
There's this black widow spider, darling, and she's been
walking on my hand.
And we've had this little heart to heart and I think I
understand.

It's a funny situation, I mean what am I to do?
With Lisa in the upstairs room and Joan and Martha too.
I can't come down to breakfast 'cause the plates have all
been used.
And it's as crowded as a subway car and I think that
you're confused.
Now I would wait at your station but I do believe it's time
that I went home.

I am at Black Widow station, darling, and I've been
waiting for your train.
I am at Black Widow station, darling, and I've been
waiting for your train.
You've been too long, darling, and it looks like rain.
You've been too long, darling, and it looks like rain.

VIDOW STATION

JUST FRIENDS

for BG

We're friends, that's all we
   are
and that's all we will
   become
It's understood
we're only friends
And it's better that way
for everyone concerned
So if you brush against me
when we're walking side
   by side
I won't wonder what
   you're thinking
'cause we've got nothing
   to hide
And I know you didn't
   mean it that way
'cause we're just friends

We're friends, that's all we
   are
and that's all we'll ever be
Is friends
And we can split the check
But we'll never bring the
   conversation
around to you and me
If I see your hand upon me
it's no reason for alarm
I realize you must have
   seen
something walking down
   my arm
And I know you didn't
   mean it that way
'cause we're just friends

Oh I know, and you know
that this is really the way
that it ought to be
'Cause if it was another way
we'd have a lot of trouble
and we'd end up in confu-
   sion
and we'd lose a lot of sleep
We both know better than
   to slip and go
and get ourselves all tan-
   gled up again
If we want to keep our
   peace of mind
we've got to keep a little
   distance
and just be friends

Oh yeah, uh huh, oh

So I'll try to understand
when I feel your arm
   around my back
That you really meant to
   do something else
but somehow you've got-
   ten off the track
'Cause I know you didn't
   mean it that way
'cause we're just friends
I know you didn't mean it
   that way
oh I know, you didn't
   mean it that way
yes I know, you didn't
   mean it that way
'cause we're just friends

st. valentine's day

It began when the moon
arrived in the mail
golden and broken in bits.
That's when I knew
that things were through
with me and you
pal.

I went back to the party
to steal a kiss from someone
and found a trial instead.

Somewhere far away in another state
a man was murdered
his throat cut and the jury is out
they say it was suicide
but we know better.
how does a man cut his own throat?
especially on Valentine's Day . . .

tulips

Of all the flowers that you sent
the tulips are the strangest ones.
first they wither, then they curl
their stems around the vase like snakes—
a quiet rioting of colors: old,
ominous and fluid.

They don't crumble softly, drop each petal
one by one; they don't wither and solidify
with dignity, like roses do
but scream in silence, yawn and wind
like something on Medusa's head.

So today I picked them out.
Before they opened in their
Silent shout.

the screaming pope
(thanks to francis bacon)

he is in a room
bare as a cube
sits on a throne, or a chair.
wearing his public robes
in a private place
he turns to us
opens his mouth
he is screaming.

we see his teeth.
we watch his neck.
it's the private face
of a public man.

one thing though
we don't hear what he sounds like.
if he were singing
what are his words?

no words.
he has no words.
that's why he screams.

how to make a poem

Take this language
Shake it well, subdue it
Hold it, keep it still.
Stop its wiggling.
Club it. Then
Gouge it, smooth it.
Shape, hollow it out.
Point it and make it sharp
Hollow, smooth, and round.

RUSTED PIPE

Now the time has come to speak
I was not able
And water through a rusted pipe
Could make the sense that I do

Gurgle, mutter
Hiss, stutter
Moan the words like water
Rush and foam and choke

Having waited
This long of a winter
I fear I only
Croak and sigh

Somewhere deep within
Hear the creak
That lets the tale begin

Now the time has come to move
I was not able
Water through a rusted pipe
Could make the moves that I do

Stagger, stumble
Trip, fumble
I fear I only
Slip and slide

Somewhere deep within
Hear the creak
That lets the tale begin

Somewhere deep within
Hear the creak
That lets the tale begin

BLOOD
MAKES
NOISE

I'd like to help you, Doctor
Yes I really really would
But the din in my head
It's too much and it's no good

I'm standing in a windy tunnel
Shouting through the roar
And I'd like to give the information
You're asking for

But blood makes noise
It's a ringing in my ear
Blood makes noise
And I can't really hear you
In the thickening of fear

I think that you might want to know
The details and the facts
But there's something in my blood
Denies the memory of the acts

So just forget it, Doc.
I think it's really
cool that you're concerned
But we'll have to try again
After the silence has returned

'Cause blood makes noise
It's a ringing in my ear
Blood makes noise
And I can't really hear you
In the thickening of fear

Blood makes noise . . .

LANGUAGE

If language were liquid
It would be rushing in
Instead here we are
In a silence more eloquent
Than any word could ever
    be

These words are too solid
They don't move fast
    enough
To catch the blur in the brain
That flies by and is gone
Gone
Gone
Gone

I'd like to meet you
In a timeless, placeless
    place
Somewhere out of context
And beyond all conse-
    quences

Let's go back to the building
    (Words are too solid)
On Little West Twelfth
It is not far away
    (They don't move fast
    enough)
And the river is there
And the sun and the spaces
Are all laying low
    (To catch the blur in the
    brain)
And we'll sit in the silence
    (That flies by and is)
That comes rushing in and
    is
Gone (Gone)

I won't use words again
They don't mean what I
    meant
They don't say what I said
They're just the crust of the
    meaning
With realms underneath
Never touched
Never stirred
Never even moved
    through

If language were liquid
It would be rushing in
Instead here we are
In a silence more eloquent
Than any word could ever
    be

And is gone
Gone
Gone
And is gone

CRACKING

It's a one-time thing
It just happens
A lot
Walk with me
And we will see
What we have got
Ah. . .

My footsteps are ticking
Like water dripping from a tree
Walking a hairline
And stepping very carefully
Ah. . .

My heart is broken
It is worn out at the knees
Hearing muffled
Seeing blind
Soon it will hit the Deep Freeze

And something is cracking
I don't know where
Ice on the sidewalk
Brittle branches
In the air

The sun
Is blinding
Dizzy golden, dancing green
Through the park in the afternoon
Wondering where the hell
I have been
Ah. . .

FREEZING

(From *Songs from Liquid Days* by Philip Glass)

If you had no name
If you had no history
If you had no books
If you had no family

If it were only you
Naked on the grass
Who would you be then?
This is what he asked

And I said I wasn't really sure
But I would probably be
Cold

And now I'm freezing
Freezing

dream themes 5

for CS

they say her grip is weak
but they don't know her as I do.
they say her vision is tipped
and I would disagree
her fingertips are liquid
they run over your shoulder
down across your elbow
and drip from your wrist
and if you ever thought
you ever had the power
now how could you resist.

she says the disease makes her tired
that her fingers are dissolving
like icicles in sun
but she laughs and you can tell that
her eyes are burnt with fever
and you know that though she's sick
that she has won.

angel is burning

for PB in a fever

All bone and eyes
And turned down mouth
He's pale as a candle
Hot as a handful of matches

You cradle the thing you touch
What do you feel you deserve?
Angel has a fever.

We watch him upon his knees
He's thin as a candle
His forehead is a flame.

The angel is burning
with a fever of 104
His clothes are falling
We are on the floor

The angel is up there
so pale he's melting away
We're holding you up there
we will not let you fall
all your flesh has fallen away

He is in love
but not with you
and not with me.

99.9F°

**99.9 Fahrenheit degrees
Stable now, with rising possibilities
It could be normal but it isn't quite
Could make you want to stay awake at night**

**You seem to me
Like a man
On the verge of burning
99.9 Fahrenheit degrees**

Pale as a candle
And your face is hot
And if I touch you
I might get what you've got

You seem to me
Like a man
On the verge of running
99.9 Fahrenheit degrees

Something cool
Against the skin
Is what you could be
Something cool
Against the skin
Is what you
Could be needing

99.9 Fahrenheit degrees

You seem to me
Like a man
On the verge of burning
99.9 Fahrenheit degrees

Something cool
Against the skin
Is what you could be
Something cool
Against the skin
Is what you
Could be needing

99.9 Fahrenheit degrees
99.9 Fahrenheit degrees

FIFTY–FIFTY CHANCE

Fifty-fifty chance
The doctor said
In the cardiac room
As she's lying in bed

There's a pan on the floor
Filled with something black
I need to know
I'm afraid to ask

I hug you
I hum to you
I've come to you
I touch you

I tell you
I love you
I sing to you
Bring to you
anything

Her little heart
It beats so fast
Her body trembles
With the effort to last

I hug you
I hum to you
I've come to you
I touch you

I tell you
I love you
I sing to you
Bring to you
anything

She's going home
Tomorrow at ten
The question is
Will she try it again?

Annamarie when she
Dreams at night
Removes her face
From that side of her head.

She does it for safety.
In case someone sees her
And calls her to get
Out of bed.

We will dance
On a stage
In a cage
Of her bones
In the sunset of her
Diseased mouth.

Somewhere, up
And to the right,
is something like
A deep scar.
But she knows that some-
    thing was left
in the skin, in the flesh
Still there,
Under the healing.

Something sore.
Something raw.
Something hard
Something still feeling.

She said that she saw
Her face splintered and
    passed
From family to family
To family

This one the eyes,
that one the nose
But she's stuck with most
Of the history.

But some things caught fire
And were lost
As they fell through the
    cracks.

Annamarie
Only thinks of her face
As being the outside of her
    head.

She doesn't know
That it's how the world
Apprehends her
Understands her.

If you don't like the song
    that I sing
Then don't ever sing it at
    home.
Don't sing in the hallway
    from kitchen to bath-
    room
But think of it when you're
Alone.

annamarie

gunpowder

Her family
lay like gunpowder
latent and scattered
through the land
a suicide here
an overdose there.

He was the fire
focused, intense
that set off the explosion
that was our family.

In my dreams
we are all together still
he still explains
with an open hand
that we have to let go.

And I'm trying to explain
It doesn't work that way . . .

PILGRIMAGE

This line is burning
Turning to ash as it hits the
air
Every step is a day in the
week
It's a Sunday or Monday
A march over months of
the year

This life is burning
Turning to ash as it hits the
air
Every death is an end in
the race
It's a stopping and starting
A marching over millions
of years

Travel. Arrival.
Years of an inch and a
step
Toward a source
I'm coming to you
I'll be there in time

This land is burning
Turning to ash as it hits the
air
Every line is a place on a
map
It's a city or valley
A mark on these miles of
fields

Travel. Arrival.
Years of an inch and a
step
Toward a source
I'm coming to you
I'll be there in time

This line is burning
Turning to ash as it hits the
air
Every step is a day in the
week
It's a Wednesday or
Thursday
A march over months of
the year

Take this
Mute mouth
Broken tongue.
Now this
Dark life
Is shot through with light.

Travel. Arrival
Years of an inch and a
step
Toward a source
I'm coming to you
I'll be there in time

I'm coming to you
I'll be there in time

BLOOD SINGS

When blood sees blood
Of its own
It sings to see itself again
It sings to hear the voice it's known
It sings to recognize the face

One body split and passed along the line
From the shoulder to the hip
I know these bones as being mine
And the curving of the lip

And my question to you is
How did this come to pass?
How did this one life fall so far and fast?

Some are lean and some with grace, and some without;
All tell the story that repeats
Of a child who had been left alone at birth
Left to fend and taught to fight

See his eyes and how they start with light
Getting colder as the pictures go
Did he carry his bad luck upon his back?
That bad luck we've all come to know

And my question to you is:
How did this come to pass?
How did this one life fall so far and fast?

When blood sees blood
Of its own
It sings to see itself again
It sings to hear the voice it's known
It sings to recognize the face

BIRTH-DAY (LOVE MADE REAL)

one thing I know
this pain will go

step through all that's left to feel
I wait to meet my love made real

don't move don't touch
don't talk so much

strip and find the place to kneel
I wait to meet my love made real

one thing I know
this day will go

don't touch don't talk crawl the wall
she's the ticket to the future don't listen down the hall
you can say your prayer to the head of this bed
when it begins at your knees and goes right to your
   head

birth-day

strap me down from wrist to heel
I wait to meet my love made real

one thing I know
this day will go

shake all over like an old sick dog
there's a needle here needle there tremble in the fog
it's a tight squeeze vice grip ice and fire
she's a hot little treasure and the wave goes higher

birth-day
birth-day

Somewhere in a room
With a poster on a wall
Of a man with his hand
In a fist

Is a woman who's drinking
And her dress is so tight
You can see every breath
That she takes

Every sigh, every sway
You can hear everything that they say
Something's begun like a war
Or a family or a friendship
Or a fast love affair

The man on the wall
Is his symbol of freedom
It means he has brothers
Who believe as he does

ROOM
OFF THE
STREET

She is moved by
The thing that she sees in his face
When he talks of
The cause

Every sigh, every sway
You can hear everything that they say
Something's begun like a war
Or a family or a friendship
Or a fast love affair

She leans against him
Her dress is so red
They talk of the salt
And the truth and the bread

The night goes along
The fan goes around
In the room off the street
At the end of the town

Every sigh, every sway
You can hear everything that they say
Something's begun like a war
Or a family or a friendship
Or a fast love affair

my friend is an old cat

for JMP

On my wedding day
I went to see my friend
Who was making
My wedding dress.

The fitting the day before
Had gone very badly.
The dress would not close over my bosom.
And it's not a very large bosom
So now you know
How badly it went.

But on this morning
It fits, all butter and cream
Sailing down my waist
And over my hips

She stood in the doorway
Smiling good-bye
Like an old cat
With her whiskers drooping over
Her upper lip, this Friday morning
In the sun.

promise

Take this word
Wind it twice around your heart
Once to hold it together
And again,
So it won't come apart.

HONEYMOON SUITE

the ceiling had a painting on it
in our room in France
so we were living underneath
some angels in a dance

my husband was not feeling well
and so we went to bed
he woke up complaining
of an aching in his head

he said a hundred people
had come through our room that night
that one by one the old and young
asked if he was all right

one by one the old and young
lined up to touch his hand
he spent the night explaining
they had come to the wrong man

the concierge was less than helpful
when we asked her the next day
with coffee and a magazine
we went to the desk to pay

"what happened in that room?" he asked
"a death or something strange?"
she smiled at him politely
and returned to him his change

well, what I'd like to know
and this will be a mystery,
is with all the people in that room
why none appeared to me?

when we sleep so close together that
our hair becomes entwined
I must have missed that moment
in the gateway to his mind

WORLD BEFORE COLUMBUS

If your love were taken from me
Every color would be black and white
It would be as flat as the world before Columbus
That's the day that I lose half my sight

If your life were taken from me
All the trees would freeze in this cold ground
It would be as cruel as the world before Columbus
Sail to the edge and I'd be there looking down

Those men who lust for land
And for riches strange and new
Who love those trinkets of desire
Oh they never will have you

And they'll never know the gold
Or the copper in your hair
How could they weigh the worth
Of you so rare

If your love were taken from me
Every light that's bright would soon go dim
It would be as dark as the world before Columbus
Down the waterfall and I'd swim over the brim

Those men who lust for land
And for riches strange and new
Who love those trinkets of desire
Oh they will never have you

And they'll never know the gold
Or the copper in your hair
How could they weigh the worth
Of you so rare

LEAF SONG

by Suzanne and Alyson Vega
(Ages 14 and 11)

I am a leaf
on a tree by the river
in this house of more
than just pigeon feather
I don't care when I die
Who would?
Man, not a leaf, not I

We live here together
all sister, all brother
who cares when we're older
like father, like mother?
we dream of a life
where we move by means
other than the wind

We dream of a life
where we move by means
other than the wind . . .

And we all would fall
but for shelter and beauty
which one among us
will be the first in the family
who will go traveling
further than sister like mine?

We dream of a life
where we move by means
other than the wind

I am a leaf
on a tree by the river
in this house of more
than just pigeon feather

I don't care when I die
Who would?
Man, not a leaf like I . . .

Sonny boy, you need new sneakers
Better go into town and get them Friday night
Come to think of it, kid, you need just about everything
But I think things are gonna be all right,
Yes, I think things are gonna be all right.

So you went and got yourself back into trouble
Went and got yourself into another fight
Come on here, let me see your eye, now it's all black
   and swollen
But I think you're gonna be all right
Yes, I think that you're gonna be all right.

I don't know why you're such a troublemaker
You'd think that maybe by now you'd see the light
Getting yourself torn up, boy, and we don't have that
   much money
But I think maybe things will be all right,
Yes, I think maybe things will be all right.

Now maybe I shouldn't yell
'Cause I know you're just a kid
But I can't always tell
What's on your mind, half of the time, brother mine.

Now I know that you're just my little brother
And I don't expect you to get everything just right
But I think you ought to use a little more sense than
   what you're using
And maybe then things would be all right,
Yes, and maybe then things would be all right.

I know that I sit and I worry too much
Especially when you come home such a sight
But I guess what you've got to do, boy, you go ahead
   and do it
And I sure hope things will be all right,
Yes, I sure hope things will be all right.

Now you come back here, you scruffy little brother
Come on back here and let me kiss you good night
'Cause I know if you were gone I'd miss the sound of
   laughter
And that's gonna make everything all right,
Yes, that's gonna make everything all right.

BROTHER MINE
(Age 14)

NIGHT VISION

Thanks to Paul Eluard

By day give thanks
By night beware
Half the world in sweetness
The other in fear

When the darkness takes you
With her hand across your face
Don't give in too quickly
Find the thing she's erased

Find the line, find the shape
Through the grain
Find the outline, things will
Tell you their name

The table, the guitar
The empty glass
All will blend together when
Daylight has passed

Find the line, find the shape
Through the grain
Find the outline, things will
Tell you their name

Now I watch you falling into sleep
Watch your fist uncurl against the sheet
Watch your lips fall open and your eyes dim
In blind faith

I would shelter you
Keep you in light
But I can only teach you
Night vision
Night vision
Night vision

cold blue steel

childhood was the forge
in which this character
was hammered out,
a place of unbearable heat,
flames,
either molten and raw,
or cold blue steel,
to be hammered on
until you give way.

the sword

He said, "We are making
the perfect sword
and for this we need
the perfect furnace.
We work at night
to watch the flame
temper the steel."

At first I thought
I wanted the sword.
Then I saw
I was the sword.

trial by fire

Trial by fire
what will we find?
Gold? or only ashes?
After the sifting
And scattering's done
Will we find any flashes?

dream themes

Here is a girl
who has removed her face
with the sharpest thing around
that she could find
she used your tongue
against her cheek
the gentlest blade.

We all stood
inside the glass cathedral
watching as the wind outside
blew dirty hot and wide
and as it slowly passed
over the people left outside
they shuddered and they slowly
turned away and put their
faces in their hands.

A woman on her knees
with her skirts in the dirt
her wrists were strapped across
with a rope made of pearls
She said take them please
just leave me here
and then she said no more

I rode upon a horse
Made of a strong white beauty
And a crowd parted as we rode through
I was lucky and proud and strong and humble
Because it wasn't mine.
And yet it carried me.
So we both were free.

Here's a girl who died in the night of a headache
Though the picture shows just where the bullet lies
And a boy who's ribs are made of fragile glass
He only stood amazed and stunned when the blow came.
No anger. Just the crash.

Here's the gardener who's buried
beneath the garden.
And right where he lies
Is where the garden grows the best.

pearl of fear—
dream theme 4

she appeared again that night
as she so often does
and said, "Nobody dies
from diving for pearls."

And in the word "pearl"
Hid the word "fear"
With the "l" crossed out
and the "p" scraped away.

PEARL

break the haven

One hand on the knob
of a door that's closed—
I will open it wide.
And throw inside
What I hold in this hand.

What I hold in this hand
Are the gems that burn
And drip with flame
I will throw them in
They will spread like fire.

Someone's room will
Be consumed.
And I will tell you why.
I'm breaking the haven.

Burning tight against the skin
I'll throw them in.
They will spread like prayer.

Today I am
A small blue thing
Like a marble
Or an eye

With my knees against my mouth
I am perfectly round
I am watching you

I am cold against your skin
You are perfectly reflected
I am lost inside your pocket
I am lost against
Your fingers

I am falling down the stairs
I am skipping on the sidewalk
I am thrown against the sky

I am raining down in pieces
I am scattering like light
Scattering like light
Scattering like light

Today I am
A small blue thing
Made of china
Made of glass

I am cool and smooth and curious
I never blink
I am turning in your hand
Turning in your hand
Small blue thing

SMALL BLUE THING

desire

You are my
dark jewel, my
Amethyst, my
purple deep, you are
Dark like plums.

MY FAVORITE PLUM

My favorite plum
hangs so far from me
See how it sleeps
and hear how it calls to me
See how the flesh
presses the skin,
It must be bursting
with secrets within,
I've seen the rest, yes
and that is the one for me

See how it shines
it will be so sweet
I've been so dry
it would make my heart complete
See how it lies
languid and slow
Never noticing
me here below
I've seen the best, yes
and that is the one for me

Maybe a girl will take it
Maybe a boy will steal it
Maybe a shake of the bough
will wake it and make it fall

My favorite plum
lies in wait for me
I'll be right here
longing endlessly
You'll say that I'm
foolish to trust
But it will be mine
and I know that it must
'cause I've had the rest, yes
and that is the one for me
I've seen the best, yes
and that is the one for me

red bean

in Japan
is a girl
who knows
how a boy becomes
a man.

sweet red bean
on ice
soaked in milk
and worth the price.

in the world
of the salary man
she sits apart.
no one knows
what's in her heart.

a cherry in
a dish of cream.
who knows what
these visions mean?

CARAMEL

It won't do
to dream of caramel,
to think of cinnamon
and long for you.

It won't do
to stir a deep desire,
to fan a hidden fire
that can never burn true.

I know your name,
I know your skin,
I know the way
these things begin;

But I don't know
how I would live with myself,
what I'd forgive of myself
if you don't go.

So good-bye,
sweet appetite,
no single bite
could satisfy . . .

I know your name,
I know your skin,
I know the way
these things begin;

But I don't know
what I would give of myself,
how I would live with myself
if you don't go.

It won't do
to dream of caramel,
to think of cinnamon
and long
for you.

hunger strike
for RM

"You're so thin," he said. "You're incredibly frail."

I looked at him and felt a little afraid and very alert. I was not used to being naked before him. He lay on the bed, smoking a cigarette, and I sat in his chair. I picked up my skirt from the floor and held it, bunched in my hands—I was beginning to feel cold.

"You're so thin," he said, "that if I were to make love to you you would break in half like a twig."

I sat poised on the chair, like a bird about to take flight, frightened and watchful. I wasn't sure quite what was going on yet.

"You're so thin," he said, watching me with serious eyes, "that they should open a fund for you, to feed the Starving Child. You look like a little girl. It hurts me to look at you. It's amazing. You look like you're almost all bone—"

"Can't you at least wait until I have all my clothes back on?" I said quietly, beginning to feel a small pain inside. He was quiet, and I could feel him looking at me, in the dark light of the candle burning in the corner. He looked startled, laughed, and then grew serious again.

"I mean, you're beautiful," he said. "You're sort of—perfect. You're so fragile."

"Thank you," I said, and began to put on my shirt.

"Wait a second. Come here. Don't put that on yet."

I went over to him, and he put his arms around me as I got onto the bed next to him. The bed was by the window, and since the light was off, he had the shades up, and I could see all the rooftops, all the lights, the river, the sky—the city stretched out for miles—and it seemed like a different land to me. It was what Europe must be like, I thought. So much strangeness. I hardly recognized the streets below, even though I lived all my life on them—just as I hardly recognized Jeff's face in this strange dark flickering light, though we'd been friends for a long time.

I curled up against him and put the blanket over both of us, and we looked out the window.

"So why are you so skinny? Don't you eat?"

"Yes, I eat. You've seen me eat. You saw me eat last week when we went out for breakfast."

"Last week? Is that the last time?"

"No, it's not the last time I ate. I ate breakfast this morning."

"Is that all?"

I didn't say anything else but I curled up against him for the heat. I didn't feel like eating. The thought of it made me sick, and yet I almost always feel the pangs sharp in my stomach. That morning I had thrown away most of what was on my plate—the eggs with their greasy softness and the butter, melting into the bread, made me feel suddenly disgusted and queasy.

"So what are we going to do?" I said to him.

"I don't know." he said. "I don't know if this is such a good idea. I mean, at least one of us is likely to get hurt."

I agreed with him.

"What are you trying to do? Starve yourself to get back at him? And what am I supposed to do when you two get back together? I'm worried. I'm leaving myself wide open . . ."

He flicked his ashes.

"I think maybe I should put my clothes back on, don't you think?"

He held me closer to him.

"No, not just yet. I've never made love to such a frail little woman. I'm leaving myself open. But I know loveliness when I've got it."

He stared at me, serious and friendly now, and I was happy that we were friends, even though I wasn't sure if I wouldn't rather put my clothes back on, now that we'd both balked at this opportunity. I wasn't used to this. Usually we were buddies—we were on equal ground, sparring and quarreling and arguing. There was no question of surrendering, only the tenderness of acknowledging a rival as an equal. That is, we both knew when to back off, and that in itself was a sort of tenderness. To be in his arms naked was too strange.

And I didn't want to fall in love with him, fall into the burning pit that sapped all my strength and shook me down to the roots, tearing at my stomach. I had enough trouble.

"You take too much onto yourself," Jeff said. "You're goddamned arrogant. You have too much hubris, whatever the hell it is—you think you can deal with everything. Well, there's a breaking point. You're too skinny. I don't know what you're trying to change by not eating—are you going to put your death on his conscience? Are you fasting to death in front of him?"

"I don't know what to say."

"I think he's a fool. I don't know why he'd go running around with other women when he had you. He's nuts. And so are you. And so am I."

I wasn't sure what I was trying to do, myself. I felt so lonely, and so bitter sometimes and before I'd broken up with him I wanted so desperately for him to look at me the way he had in the beginning, and then it became apparent that he was seeing other women.

And the helplessness began, and the crying every afternoon, when I would get home, and the warm orange sun of late afternoon shone down across the bed, and I would think about how it had been at the beginning, the giddy joyous feelings, and the peace I felt when he was in my arms and happy there, and I thought about how cold it felt now, and I would feel so bitter . . . and I thought of that other woman's face, that one time when I met her, and she was so self-assured and I thought how she must pity me, and I wanted to hurt her in a way I've never felt since. I would have hit her.

But I didn't. We were in public, I watched as he went over to her and made plans for dinner with her, and I had the feeling of being caught in an awful cycle of breaking up and coming together and breaking up . . . and then soon after I just didn't feel like eating anymore.

I had some idea that if I were strong, if I were hard and compact, it would be okay. I wanted to be brilliant like a diamond, tight like a fist. Compact like a bullet. My hips nauseated me, my thighs made me helplessly furious with their looseness, and I had the feeling that crying could wear me down, wear me thin with salt water, salting down the flesh, smoothing down to the bone, and I would be light and free.

I felt so hungry finally that I could not eat. Hungry for affection, for attention, for food and warmth—I wanted it all so badly that I couldn't accept it, like the hunger strikers who threw up even water because their small stomachs couldn't take it. Instead of being compact like steel girders, I was becoming brittle, like those men who were so thin that their bones were in danger of breaking through the skin, the skin stretched taut against their faces . . .

"Your face looks almost sculpted," he said. "Your skin goes right across your cheekbones. It's incredible. Look at your tiny wrist here . . ."

"Shut up," I said. "If you don't I'll tell you about the hunger strikers who turn black from hunger, how they put one on a waterbed to keep him from hurting himself, how the body eats up all the fat and then starts on the muscle tissue, consuming itself . . ."

He started to look horrified.

"All right." he said. "Keep being a martyr. I don't know. I just wish I didn't care about you. But we'd be terrible for each other. I don't think I could take too much of you. Go on, put your clothes on, and then come back in here, and we'll go out for breakfast again in the morning."

DOPAMINE

(From *Dopamine*, solo album by Mitchell Froom)

it's what you wish for
what you haven't had
what you think of
when you're feeling bad

feel the pull
it's what you want
in a chemical

it rearranges
the inside of your brain
feel the weight of
the neurological chain
could be coffee
could be cocaine

feel the pull
it's what you want
in a chemical

too much
and you feel bizarre
join the rats here
and bang on the bar

feel the pull
it's what you want
in a chemical

talking

You make me feel
Hungry
And I've been
Full for a while

Now it feels
Strange to be
Hungry again
And hungry for what?

I want to rub against
your mind
I want to hold
Every idea
You have ever had

I love your body
Because your mind is shining
through it
Sounds weird
But I think that's what
It is

I'm hungry for company
And laughing in the night
I think that's it
Hungry for novelty
Melody, rhyme
And reason, I guess

But mostly for talking
your startling words
that stir up my feelings
like birds

UNDERTOW

I believe right now if I could
I would swallow you whole
I would leave only bones and teeth
We could see what was underneath
And you would be free then

Once I thought only tears could make us free
Salt wearing down to the bone
Like sand against the stone
Against the shoreline

I am friend to the undertow
I take you in, I don't let go
And now I have you

I wanted to learn all the secrets
From the edge of a knife
From the point of a needle
From a diamond
From a bullet in flight
I would be free then

I am friend to the undertow
I take you in, I don't let go
And now I have you

I wanted to see how it would feel
To be that sleek
And instead I find this hunger's
Made me weak

I believe right now if I could
I would swallow you whole
I would leave only bones and teeth
We could see what was underneath
And you would be free then

I am friend to the undertow
I take you in, I don't let go
And now I have you

I am friend to the undertow
I take you in, I don't let go
And now I have you

SALT WATER

(From *Taste This* by DNA)

Tide came in
And then went out
And left behind
In hollow places
Cradled once
And cooling twice
You feel the sting of

Salt water

Wave goes back
And leaves the sand
It's high and barren
Dry and wasting
Cradled once
And cooling twice
You feel the sting of

Salt water

Taste this
It's really raw
It comes with the skin
And the sand still on it
And it comes with the shell
And the flesh within it
You can tell that it came
From a seedy and watery place

Taste this
It's really good
It will make your mouth
Feel like something's in it
And it's gotten and given
From a cold black piece of the sea

From a piece of the sea

Salt water

dirty birth

Today I ate three razor clams. Hollow
Long tubes, open, each half
a straight razor. Holding a prize inside.
They tasted murky, like brine
From the deepest forgotten
Corner of the ocean.
They were good. Salty
Fat worms, musty and exposed.
Gotten and given from
The groin, from a seedy and watery place
Carrying traces of their sandy
Dirty birth.

clean

I will wash
my neck and ears
Remove all jewelry.
Soak until
I am clean enough
for you to kiss.

dream theme 4

We lay on the hill
packed up the stars
the moon
the sun and the stun
of the kiss on the slope

thrill of a small fall

for AM

Foolish girl
To be so
Impressed by a kiss
Something stolen and sweet
Listen to how she's
Going on like this

Come here now
Give me the thrill
Of a small fall
You've got me again
Caught me on
Something familiar.

celadon

for GB

you are in
the celadon green
of each tin
house I pass

on my way
to pray
your thin brown
hand with the vein
arises before my eyes

and the one day
so far away
when you held my foot
in your hungry hand

I didn't know then
that you would still stay
and be with me in the land I move through

and that I would
wish for your touch
all day every day
I've known you so long after all.

haiku

(Age 11)

Peace is part of love
But love is not all peaceful
It can be quite fierce.

GYPSY

You come from far away
With pictures in your eyes
Of coffeeshops and morning streets
In the blue and silent sunrise

But night is the cathedral
Where we recognized the sign
We strangers know each other now
As part of the whole design

Oh, hold me like a baby
Who will not fall asleep
Curl me up inside you
And let me hear you through the heat

You are the jester of this courtyard
With a smile like a girl's
Distracted by the women
With the dimples and the curls

By the pretty and the mischievous
By the timid and the blessed
By the blowing skirts of ladies
Who promise to gather you to their breast

Oh, hold me like a baby . . .

You have hands of raining water
And that earring in your ear
The wisdom on your face
Denies the number of your years

With the fingers of the potter
And the laughing tale of the fool
The arranger of disorder
With your strange and simple rules

Yes now I've met me another spinner
Of strange and gauzy threads
With a long and slender body
And a bump upon the head

Oh, hold me like a baby . . .

With a long and slender body
And the sweetest softest hands
And we'll blow away forever soon
And go on to different lands

And please do not ever look for me
But with me you will stay
And you will hear yourself in song
Blowing by one day

Oh, hold me like a baby . . .

compass

When I am with you
The needle goes north . . .

unfinished

For the Gaudi Cathedral in Barcelona

We stood in front of the cathedral.
They call it an unfinished symphony of
Steel and stone.
A million pigeons moved,
And the stone began to breathe.

We felt its longing to be completed.
It yearned into the sky.
We stood in front
And it was our yearning too.

Together now in the dark
Before we fall asleep
We'll finish it here.

bird on a mountain

for AS

I said to you
as we lay together—
I stretch out as far as I can
in either direction
and there's always more of you.

You said, with your eyes lit up—
Remember when you said
You were like a bird on
A mountain, or a vine
On a tree?

tuesday morning

Run your finger
over my lips
I am melting
Like sugar in a burning spoon
I can tell by the way you touch me
You've had children
Handled little bundles
of the skin and the bone.

burning
burden

Lying
with my face
on that floor
in that room
on that night,
I carried the burning burden
Ever after

I carried it
in my arms and it burned my
Chest and shoulders.

It was more than just
A woman's love
Though it burned in my breast
Too.

Now I know
It's not just me
But all of you
Who tremble too.

key to the kingdom
for MF

as though I learned to see
and to speak of what I saw
although there is no word
for that which I know now

we had passed through a threshold
where nothing was the same
but still it was familiar
as the sound of my own name

like light and like color
like hunger and like pain
a wanting and a having
all together

I will do
what I can do
for you
for you

cremation

There's a graveyard in Tokyo
Without any graves
In the middle of the city
In the middle of the night.

You had returned from a pain of your own
And were back.

All the stones
So close together.
It made me wonder
Are they still standing?

Standing up forever
Like in the subway.
They must be very tired.
No rest for these dead.

TOMBSTONE

I like a tombstone 'cause it
weathers well
and if it stands or if it crumbles
only time will tell

if you carve my name in marble
you must cut it deep
there'll be no dancing on the gravestone
you must let me sleep
and time is burning burning burning
it burns away

I don't need to see the gates of
famous men
but I do try to see the kingdom
every now and then

if you ask me where it is it's on a
humble map
and I know that to enter in the doorway
show your handicap
and time is burning burning burning
it burns away

the happy gravedigger

My daughter Ruby and I went over the hill on Sunday to see the pretty lit-
tle cemetery by the side of the road. We walked up and down the rows of
graves, and noticed one for "Ruby Sybil." Another was for the unfortunate-
ly named "Fanny Anny Butt," who was buried there with the whole Butt
family. There were graves to the right of us, and graves to the left, and ivy
on the stones. It was mild weather, but there was in the sky that mixture
of sun shafts and gray clouds that is common to England, especially out
here in the country.

We saw the caretaker of the graves and the chapel—a small man with a
tight overcoat, white hair, a grizzled beard and ready smile.

"Are you American? Oh, you look just like us, then!" he said, surprised
to hear my accent. "The little one's name is Ruby?" His eyes flickered over
to Ruby Sybil's grave but he didn't mention it. "Ruby! Ruby, don't take your
love to town! Kenny Rogers and the First Edition!"

He laughed. Ruby looked at him gravely and did not smile.

"Your hair is a lovely color. Mine was that color. Auburn, do you call it?
I hated it to be called ginger. It was auburn, and stood up in right curls!
What's her hair like, then? Not so red."

I told him that I could see bits of this auburn still visible in his beard. His
face lit up at the thought that there was still color left, and he put his fin-
gers up as though he could feel the dark reddish color itself. He told me he
was fifty-four, and this surprised me, for I thought he was at least seventy,
from the state of his teeth and his craggy face.

He told me of the two christenings he was going to, and how he was
going to drive into London; told me he had lost a son who had been twenty-
six years old, to drugs and drink, in Bath, up the road, and how painful it was.

"Although I think that these people have gone to a better place.
Don't you think that is a good idea? I don't know if it is true, but I like the
idea. I like the idea that when I die, I will meet my son in a better place.

Do you believe in God?" he asked, looking at me anxiously.

Well, yes I do, sometimes, but not in any formal organized sense, I told him. This seemed to satisfy him.

"Yes. I like the idea that everyone is resting now. It is very peaceful here. I find it so. Why should I go anywhere else? I go to London but I will always come back here.

"Three good things have come out of America. Ford, because he made good cars; Elvis Presley, there will never be another one; and Bob Dylan. Yes! My sister, she says to come and visit her in California, near Mexico. She says that if I come and see her, we can drive round and look at all the gates of the mansions of famous people, of Frank Sinatra, and Rod Stewart.

"Well, why do I need to do that? I've got my own gates right here! Don't I? You're important, I'm important. I've got my own gates right here, I have. I don't need to go there."

He asked me, "How do they conduct the funerals there? Do they do it by hand or machine? I do everything here—tend the graves, dig them, the undertaking, ride in the hearse, all of it. The fresh graves are here, see, on the side. There is always work!"

I had to tell him I had no idea how they dug the graves in America. "You don't know? So you haven't been to a funeral recently then? Well, you are still young. I lost my son at twenty-six. You are not much older than that, are you? I've heard they have huge caskets.

"If I were to go to America, I would like to see the truck stops, where the truckers drink coffee, eat a simple meal, attend a funeral. Simple things. That's what I would like."

This notion pleased him. He asked for my name, and when I told him what it was, he said, "My daughter has the same name as you, spelled the same. Will you go into the chapel and sign your name? Thank you!"

I left him in his little house on the grounds, and as we walked home, I felt that he was one of the most cheerful men I had ever met.

thin man (poem)

Though he is not my friend
Lately I feel my death with me.
He looks over my shoulder
Presses against the back of my neck,
When I step off the curb
He steps with me.
He laughs at any plan
I think of making,
showing his fine white teeth.
He thinks I'm funny.

THIN MAN

He is not my friend, but he is with me
Like a shadow is with a foot that falls
His hand is on my back when I step from the sidewalk
Or when I'm walking down these darkened halls

He's the Thin Man
With a date for me
To arrive at some point
I don't know when it will be

I can feel his eyes when I don't expect him
In the backseat of a taxi down Vestry Street
His arm is around my waist and he pulls me to him
He whispers things into my ear that sound so sweet

He's the Thin Man
With a date for me
To arrive at some point
I don't know when it will be

He is not my friend, but he is with me
And he promises a peace I never knew
I cannot give in, no, I must refuse him
But could I really be the one to resist that kiss so true

He's the Thin Man
With a date for me
To arrive at some point
I don't know when it will be

PREDICTIONS

Let's tell the future
Let's see how it's been done.
By numbers. By mirrors. By water.
By dots made at random on paper.

By salt. By dice.
By meal. By mice.
By dough of cakes.
By sacrificial fire.

By fountains. By fishes.
Writing in ashes.
Birds. Herbs.
Smoke from the altar.

A suspended ring or the mode of laughing
Pebbles drawn from a heap
One of these things
Will tell you something.

Let's tell the future
Let's see how it's been done.
By dreams. By the features. By letters.
By dropping hot wax into water.

By nails reflecting the rays of the sun.
By walking in a circle.
By red hot iron.
By passages in books.
A balanced hatchet.

A suspended ring or the mode of laughing
Pebbles drawn from a heap
One of these things
Will tell you something.

Let's tell the future
Let's see how it's been done.
How it's been done.

angel

how do you measure
what somebody suffers?
in droplets, in teacups,
a kilo, a pound;

and why does an angel
have wings on his shoulders?
'cause that is where the weight
of the world can be found.

the pianist
(Age 15)
for JP

music player
          cathedral builder
                    spirit sailor
you touch forth the breath
of ageless life . . . and I soar!

you give me sky
and light
ancient towering castles
sorrowful pounding glories
all battles won and lost
fill this vast place when you play
and you
have brought me
          joy . . .

the pianist

She always sat in the same place. Every morning at 8:20, she came out and sat on the floor, in the front of the dance studio, before the class began. Not directly in front—always to the left, but close enough so the teacher could not avoid seeing her, and she could see herself in the mirror.

The class always began the same way. The music would begin, and the breathing exercises would start. When there was no pianist, all that could be heard was the dry rhythm of the teacher's voice, shrill in the morning air, calling "One, two, three, four . . .," steady and monotonous. Victoria didn't mind that so much. On those days, she withdrew into her own thoughts, lulled by the rhythm, which was like the dripping of a leak on a rainy day. But when there was a bad pianist, nothing was worse. The bored ones played their boredom into the air where it hung thick like fog, and there were even some who played silly marching band music to every exercise, which made her muscles bristle with impatience.

Today James Sullivan was at the piano. Victoria had heard him play before for another class, and she had stopped in front of the closed door to listen more carefully. Later she found out who he was. His music had fascinated her, and she was curious about him. She stole a glance at his face as the music began, and he was humming the melody to himself as played, something he was improvising.

Victoria enjoyed the warm-up more than any other part of the class. She liked the solitude of each dancer working within her own space, and no one speaking to her. Once the class stood up she had to work harder for the teacher to notice her. Also, she could see herself in the mirror, which she did not like, though she stood there purposely to make herself look. She could see her thighs and stomach, which were too big. She knew they would never ever be right, or match her thin graceful arms because she ate too much.

It was no consolation that everyone ate too much. People said it was her age. "You go through a chubby stage at fifteen." they said. "You'll grow out of it. And you're nowhere near fat." No, except she was in her own eyes. And it was her appetite that worried her. After dinner, when the family had gone off to watch TV, she went back to the kitchen and ate, hastily wolfing down any food she could eat quickly. Handfuls of raisins, pieces of cheese, bread and butter, bread and mayonnaise, just plain bread, peanut butter straight from the jar—everything went into the endless pit until she felt sick with eating and could not eat any more. Even though her stomach would feel bloated out of proportion, her mouth craved more food, and she lay on her bed wondering if she was trying to commit suicide by bursting.

But this morning James Sullivan was at the piano, and she forgot about her stomach, and about her vow not to eat anything all day after last night's binge. She looked out the window at the rain, and when the time came to raise her arm high and turn, with her back arched and her head lifted, she imagined she was Joan of Arc, leading her troops into battle, glorious and courageous, and triumphant. And beautiful, although she had heard that Joan of Arc was not beautiful.

Victoria stole another glance at the pianist's face. Their eyes met, and he nodded to her. He would have smiled, she thought, but he was still singing softly to himself. He seemed like a child, with his little songs, and the way he amused himself while the teacher gave corrections by picking out little tunes on the high part of the piano. He did not look like a child, though. His hair was thinning, and Victoria guessed him to be in his mid-thirties. His character seemed out of place with his music, which was big and sorrowful, like ancient towering cathedrals, so sad and joyful at the same time. Like when the sun broke through on a rainy day and shone gold-streaked against the gray. Like freedom.

She felt the teacher's eye on her and froze. She tried not to be self-conscious, not to tighten up, tried to breathe freely until she strained with the effort. She listened to the music, and tried to imagine Joan of Arc again, but she couldn't.

"Victoria." said the teacher. "You have the right idea, but you should relax. You look like you're thinking very hard. Let go of your shoulders, that's it."

Victoria flushed a little as the music ended. She meant to relax. She meant to give herself freely, but something in her would not let go, unless she was dancing by herself. How could other people move without thinking about it? With other people it didn't seem to matter who the pianist was, either. They just danced, and it poured out of them. Sometimes it poured out of her, and she could feel it. And she knew she was good, and she knew she was special. It was like a light shining around her neck and shoulders, and it was unmistakable. But today it was not shining, even though Jim was there. Today she felt gray, and she was angry with herself.

After class, she found herself at the piano. She felt shy, but she wanted to talk to the pianist, to find out anything she could about him. The only thing she knew so far was his name, and that he had gone away to Sweden for a while last year.

James was putting the cover onto the piano.

"Hi." she said.

"Hi, Victoria," he said. "How are you?"

"I'm all right." she said, pleased that he knew her name. "Are you playing for our class from now on?"

"I think so." he said. "For the rest of the year, anyway. Till the spring concert."

Victoria nodded and leaned against the piano, as Jim put his music into his briefcase.

"I'm glad." she said. "I've always liked your music. I used to hear you playing for other classes, and I would stop and listen." She was too shy to say any more.

"Well, thank you, Victoria," he said, closing his briefcase.

She went on, feeling encouraged.

"I wasn't sure if you were here anymore. I thought you had gone to Sweden."

"I did go to Sweden. I go to Sweden every year. Every summer."

He stopped talking abruptly, and put on his black leather flight jacket that had been across the back of his chair. She said quickly,

"I once thought of going to Sweden."

"Have you ever been to Europe?" he asked.

"No."

"Well, don't go to Sweden first. It's beautiful, but very cold. The countryside is pretty as hell, but the people are cold. I've been there four summers now, and this was the first time anyone would say anything to me."

Victoria thought about this.

"Why do you go there?"

James sat down on the piano chair, with his jacket on, zipped tight. The class had gone to the locker room to change, and they were alone in the big wooden room, reflected in the huge mirrors on the wall. He smoothed the cover of the piano with his big hand, and thought for a moment. Still looking at his hand, he said,

"I was, how old? Twenty, the first time I went. I was in love with a singer, an opera singer. She was married and had three kids. And she went to Sweden, and I was in love with her, so I went with her. Her husband didn't like it much, so I came back. God, that was a long time ago. You know, she was almost twice my age and she was fooling around with me." He laughed.

"That's terrible," said Victoria, and immediately felt foolish.

"It's not terrible at all," he said sharply, though not directly to her. Victoria blushed. "It was very nice, except for her husband."

He was still looking at his hand. Victoria watched him. He seemed to be remembering, and the harshness went out of his face. A very long moment passed.

"So I have these sort of love-hate feelings for Sweden." he said finally. "Mostly I go because I can work there."

"What kind of work?"

"Playing for dance classes," he said, standing up. He picked up his brief-case and said, "So long, now. I have to run. I'll see you tomorrow."

"See you," she said, startled at his abruptness. She had never really spoken to him before, and she was surprised at the way he had opened up to her so quickly.

In the locker room, her friend Rosie was half-dressed already.

"Where were you?" she asked above the noise and chatter inside.

"Talking to James Sullivan," she said. Her mind felt full, and she felt like thinking this new event out.

"Oh, yeah? He plays well. I hate it when he speeds up and slows down, though. It kills me when I have to hold my leg out there like this and he slows down. I just hate it." said Rosie, stripping off her tights.

"He does that because he's emotional," said Victoria, quietly, putting her bag on one of the benches near Amy. "He gets carried away."

"Are you all right?" said Rosie, taking bobby pins from her hair. "Are you in a funny mood again? You look sort of quiet."

"Yes, I'm fine. I'm just thinking." Victoria took off her leotards slowly and said, "If you fell in love with someone and they went to Sweden, would you just go waltzing off to Sweden too?"

"I don't know. I doubt it. I don't have any money. I think I'm in love with Kenny, but I don't know if I'd go to Sweden for him. He wouldn't go there anyway. The farthest he's ever gone is Staten Island." said Rosie, laughing.

"I wonder if I'd ever go to Sweden for anybody." said Victoria. "I don't really think I could love anyone. That's very romantic, just to go off like that when you're only twenty...."

"Why? Did James Sullivan go off to Sweden?" asked Rosie.

"Yes." Victoria didn't want to talk about it anymore. She felt like this was a private story he had told her, even though he didn't act like it was.

"He's not an alcoholic, is he?" said Rosie, brushing out her hair.

"No, he's not an alcoholic!"

"I don't know why I thought he was. He has a red nose, I think. Doesn't he? I always thought, oh, he's such a good pianist, it's too bad he's an alcoholic. And he sings to himself at the piano. I think he's funny."

"Well, he's not that funny, and he's not an alcoholic." Victoria was only halfway undressed, and still moved slowly, thinking. Rosie looked at her.

"Do you have a crush on him?"

"No, I don't have a crush on him. I just like his music. He's too old. And I don't know anything about him." She threw her tights into the bag, and finally began putting her street clothes on. Rosie sat next to her and put her hand on her arm.

"Vicki, are you really okay?"

Victoria stopped moving and looked at her friend.

"Yeah, I just ate too much again last night, so I'm not eating today. Also, I don't think Miss Fripp is going to pick me for a lead part in the assembly. I just feel sad again, and I don't know why. I'll be okay. I just want to think. You should go and eat with Kenny. I'm fine. I am. Really."

"Well, just don't think too much. See you later, okay?" Rosie touched her shoulder and went out.

Victoria waited for a space at the mirror, and brushed her hair out. She would go to the library at lunchtime, and think about things or find a book. She became aware that Sandra was crying on the other side of the room, with a group of girls around her.

"What's the matter?" someone asked.

Sandra began laughing and crying at the same time.

"I feel so silly saying this," she said, "but my chest is just too big, and I feel awful doing jumps because, well, you know . . ."

She put her hand over her face and tried to stop crying. The girls stood around her looking at each other, and tried to think of what to say. China, who was completely flat-chested, said, "Hey, Sandra. I wish I had half your problems."

There was a silence, after which everyone went off into giggles. Sandra stopped crying, and looked embarrassed, saying, "I know, it's so silly to cry like that . . ."

"It's okay," said China. "I feel like crying, sometimes."

"But you're so skinny," said Sandra.

"I know. That's why," said China.

Victoria finished dressing quickly and went down to the library. Sometimes she felt like everyone, including herself, was so petty. It was so important how thin you were, how well your feet arched, how high your leg went, what a pretty line you made. She felt like she would never be perfect, and it made her sad. And she couldn't just cry it out like other people. Something in her wouldn't let it go, told her to be strong and not break down. So she carried it with her.

She thought about James Sullivan again, turning the new pieces of information over in her mind. He didn't look romantic. His hair was thinning, and his voice was slightly high-pitched, almost like a woman's. He did sing at the piano when he played, and he seemed to lose himself in a dream. The one romantic thing about the way he looked was his black leather flight jacket. But there was something wonderful about his playing.

* * *

She went home reluctantly after school. Her mother was at work, and her father was asleep in his room. Her two younger brothers were wrestling in the living room as she came in.

"Where's Daddy?" she said sharply.

The boys continued wrestling and giggling and paid her no attention. She felt her irritation rise.

"Listen to me. Where's Daddy? Is he asleep?"

"Yes, your Imperial Highness." said Marc, throwing Jonathan down to the floor.

"Stop it. Stop wrestling. Cut it out. You know, he's going to come out here and get mad if you wake him up. Stop!

She felt mute and helpless, and she really hoped her father would not wake up. Her father worked at night and napped in the late afternoon, and sometimes after her mother got home in the evening, they would argue, and their arguments seemed endless. She never understood the point of them. He would say to her sometimes, "You are just like your mother." So when they argued she felt vaguely responsible, as though she should be in there being yelled at also.

Jonathan had recovered from his crushing fall and had both hands around Marc's ankles.

"Okay, sucker, you asked for it!" he said.

Victoria felt desperate.

"Stop it!" she said in a hoarse whisper.

One of the boys had drunk a glass of milk in the living room, and the empty glass was on the table. Without thinking, Victoria took it and threw it to the floor, saying, "Damn you!" still whispering. She was shocked when it broke.

The two boys stopped.

"Ooh," said Jonathan. "Look."

With trembling fingers, she picked up the large pieces of shattered glass and threw them away in the kitchen, trying not to cry. She came back with the broom and the dustpan, ignoring the two boys, and clenching her teeth.

"She's gone crazy," Jonathan said in a voice of wonder. "I'm sitting down. She's really gone crazy."

He sat down on the sofa and folded his hands quietly in his lap, and would not look at her. Marc, who was older, said, "Aw, she hasn't gone crazy," but he also sat down on the sofa as if he weren't sure.

"You guys are idiots," she said, crossly, blinking back tears. "No, I haven't gone crazy. I'm sorry I scared you, Johnny. But you guys should listen to me!"

Please don't wake up, she thought. Please, please.

The door to her father's room swung open. She heard the creak and tiny threads of fear ran down her forearms. She finished sweeping up the bits and threw them into the garbage, trying not to be awkward so that her father would have no more reason to yell at her.

Her father's figure appeared in the doorway. He ran his eyes over the scene. The two boys were still sitting uncomfortably on the couch.

"What's going on?" he said. "Who's throwing things?"

"I did," said Vicki, bracing herself inside. "They—they were fighting, and um, I thought they would wake you ..."

Her words came out quickly and her nerves tingled. She held herself straight and swallowed hard. The last time he hit her the inside of her head rang for days. And it was strange, but if she'd ever felt like crying, she didn't then. She had just stared at him, blank and defiant, as if he were hitting someone else. This had made him more angry, and he'd hit her again, saying, "Do you think you're John Wayne?" and she knew he would hit her until she cried, and then she had. But only then, and secretly she was proud of it.

Lately she had forgotten whether he hit her because she held things inside, or whether she held things inside because he hit her.

The next morning Victoria was up early and decided to walk to school. Usually it was a half-hour bus ride, but if she walked quickly, it took her an hour. The weather was still gray and cloudy, but it wasn't raining. She was happy to leave the house early, so she could have some time to herself.

As her feet fell into the rhythm against the sidewalk, she thought about her father. He didn't hit her last night, he had only said, "Can't you control them any other way?" He seemed sad, or something. She couldn't quite put her finger on it. He paid hardly any attention to the incident, just walked over to the window and said,

"I hope it rains some more. Really hard."

And it did, it poured and thundered. Inside the house, her brothers went to their rooms and listened to the radio, while Victoria watched TV with her father. It seemed to her that he was lonely, and although she did not trust herself to say anything to him, she hoped her silent company helped a little. She didn't know why she couldn't say anything. Everything was so clumsy when she did it, whether it was talking, or dancing. Sometimes she was frightened of doing anything, because she was afraid of what would come out of her. She felt locked into a weary circle that she did not know how to get out of.

When her mother had come home last night, her parents spent a long time talking quietly. By the time Victoria was half-asleep, she wasn't sure if they weren't arguing again, she was relieved to be safe in bed. She wondered if they would break up. Sometimes she wished they would.

Her mind jumped away from that subject, abruptly, and she concentrated on the rhythm of her footsteps. The spring concert . . . she was hoping and hoping for a lead part, but she had a feeling she would not get one, and it was for the same reason she could not talk to her father. It was a little nagging feeling, a little fear, and it kept her locked in.

She was right. In a few weeks, the parts had all been assigned, and she was not picked for a lead role. She tried to bear it well, but she was tired a lot of the time, and the rehearsals were not interesting to her. The one consolation was that James Sullivan played for the rehearsals, and since she did not have much to do, she sat by him and talked to him as much as she was able to. She had made it a hobby to find out everything about him, no matter how trivial.

And she drank in his music. It was so free and triumphant, so huge, and so tender, the way all the notes fit together, rippling and towering, and echoing in the large wooden room. She wondered that no one else seemed to care about the music, or notice that it was so special.

Late one afternoon, after rehearsal, Rosie and Victoria were in the locker room changing.

"So how are you feeling, kiddo?" said Rosie.

"I feel like Death," said Victoria.

"Okay," said Rosie. "Are you eating today? Do you want to come and have a bran muffin with me? Bran muffins are okay when you're dieting, they go right through you, you know?" She smiled, and Victoria could not help smiling too.

"Sure," she said.

"You sure are spending a lot of time with that pianist," said Rosie.

"I like his music."

"You don't have a crush on him?"

"No," said Victoria. "I can't describe it. I love his music. He's really interesting. He's a little weird, actually, and I like him well enough, but I think his music is amazing. That makes me curious about him. He just lets all this stuff out, that amazing music, and he tells me all these odd things."

"Oh yeah? Like what?" said Rosie, rubbing her feet.

"Like one time—I don't know how we got onto the subject even—we were talking about God, and he told me he would like to be a good Christian. He's Irish, I think. And he said that he knew his sister didn't really believe in the eternity of life because she got very upset when their mother died. Then he started talking about the human spirit, and how people die but their spirit stays on, like Mozart. And then he got really excited, and started saying loudly, 'Are you going to tell me that Mozart is dead?' looking at me like he wanted me to answer. I wasn't going to say anything of the sort. I didn't know what to say."

"That's weird. I would be upset if my parents died, even if life is eternal," said Rosie. "But I think you should hurry up, because I'm starving."

They walked to the coffee shop together.

"Also, he doesn't really want to be a pianist, you know? He wants to be a writer," said Victoria.

"But he's a good pianist."

"I know, that's what I said! I said, 'But you're so good!' He said, 'Well, anything I do, I want to be the best at. Even if it's a file clerk, I want to be the best file clerk on the job. I'm the best pianist in this school.'"

"He said that?"

"Yep. I sort of know how he feels. I think he's the best one too. I think it is funny that he said it, but I don't think he's wrong. I want to be the best one, too; the best whatever I am. Don't you?"

"Not really. I want to make a living, but I don't want to be the *best*, I just like to dance. It feels good."

Victoria mulled this over. It seemed to explain a lot. It explained why Rosie was not so worried about being noticed, and she wasn't shy. She just said what she thought. She also moved as she felt like moving, and teachers liked her. But Victoria wanted to be great, and it only came out in flashes. That's why she admired the pianist so much; it seemed to pour out of him all the time. It was too much to explain.

"Are your parents coming next week to the concert?" said Rosie.

"I don't know. I haven't really told them about it. I don't really like what I'm doing. I think I'd rather wait until I have a better part."

Her parents might like to see her dance, she thought, but then they might also wonder why she was only in the chorus. She figured it was safer to have them stay home. Would she be upset if her parents died, even if life was eternal? She guessed so. Her mind jumped away from that subject, too. They swung into the warmth of the coffee shop, and Victoria was glad. Now they would talk about other things.

The spring concert was held in the school auditorium in the early afternoon. When they were seniors, they would rent a hall and it would be at night. It would be a much bigger affair. Even though they were only sophomores, it was still very exciting because they would perform in front of the whole school, in front of all the envious freshmen, and in front of everyone's parents. It was a debut of a sort. Victoria was very quiet in the dressing room beforehand, and she applied her makeup carefully and tried to calm the butterflies in her stomach.

"Are you okay?" said Rosie, who was very excited. Her face was radiant, and she was trying to warm up in the little space she had, swinging her legs and trying not to kick anyone.

"Yeah. You look beautiful."

"Thanks," she beamed. "I'm so nervous I could die."

"You'll be great, I know it," said Victoria, slowly. They took their places in the wings.

After it was over, she was tired. She knew that she had done the best she could. She had done everything well, had not fallen down, or missed a cue, her costume had not fallen apart, and she did not bang into anyone. She could relax. She felt almost numb in the dressing room, surrounded by the laughter, the groaning, the remembering already even though they'd just finished. Some girls got flowers, and the whole room buzzed with energy.

There was a soft tapping at the door.

"Who is it?" called several girls.

"It's James," said the pianist. A general scream went up into the air, as all the girls scrambled to cover themselves, laughing and saying, "Don't come in, don't come in!"

But he came in anyway, saying, "That was just beautiful! That was incredible! You're all wonderful!"

There was a chorus of scattered "Thank you's" and more laughing and screaming.

"James Sullivan, please *go out!*" demanded Sandra from across the room. She had hid herself in the shower, and clutched the curtains across her breasts.

"Okay, okay." he said. "But I thought you'd want to know you were all fabulous." He turned and left, still laughing.

Victoria watched from the corner, where she sat with her back to the door. It was funny of him to go bursting in here, she thought. He was so childish sometimes! Rosie was leaving early to have lunch with Kenny and her parents. Her own parents hadn't known about the concert, so she would have the whole afternoon to herself before she was due home from school. Maybe I'll go take the Staten Island ferry for the ride, she thought.

There was a little nagging feeling in her, though, and she dressed without taking off her makeup. No one took much notice of her. Remarks were said around her, complaints of aching feet and tights with runs in them, congratulations given and taken. Everything washed around her, blurring and humming into a sea of voices. She felt numb and tired.

"Good show, Vicki," said China.

"Thanks," said Victoria, as she left.

Outside she sat down on the steps in front of the side doors. She felt as though the weary circle would never break. There was no reason for China to say "Good show" when she hadn't done very much to deserve it.

The audience did not clap any harder when she took her bow—she was part of the chorus. She was faceless, and the fact droned on, and on, around and around.

A voice said "Hey, there, Victoria," and she knew it was the pianist.

"Hi, James." she said.

"It was a good concert!" he said. "How do you feel?"

"I feel fine," she said, and something in her snapped. She felt the tears begin, and she knew her mascara must have started running. She didn't want to cry in front of him, but she couldn't stop.

"Oh." he said, and took both her hands and pulled her to her feet. "What is it? What is it? It's okay...."

"I feel so—" She broke it off and could not continue.

"I can't," she said. "I can't seem to—I won't ever—I hate being in the chorus. I hate it so much. I want—I want ..."

She laid her head against his jacket, and felt the cool smooth black leather against her flushed face.

"Oh, no," she said, and she felt like she would never stop crying. She was deeply afraid of how hard she was crying, as though something would unscrew somewhere down in the deepest part of her and go rattling around forever, bouncing off of her inner walls. He held her, and he stroked her hair, saying,

"It's okay. You'll learn. You will. You're good. I know you are. I know how hard you work. You'll learn to be part of the chorus, and you'll be better than that. You'll learn how to give, and then you won't be in the chorus anymore...."

She began to feel an end to the crying, and she felt shy and foolish, but she kept her face against his jacket. A sense of relief began to steal over her as she listened to him talking, and a little ray of hope stirred in her. At last the circle began to break, and she thought she understood what his music had said all along.

job

It's my job
To show you wonder
To peel back days, undress minutes
And remind you of the time
Before you knew so much.
It's my job
To tickle you to thinking
To show you strangers
In those you know best.
It's my job
To remind you to pray
To bring you religion
On a Wednesday afternoon
I'm like an accident, and
Nothing less than a miracle
Will do.

BOOK OF DREAMS

In my book of dreams
In my book of dreams
In my book of dreams

I took your urgent whisper
Stole the arc of a white wing
Rode like foam on the river of pity
Turned its tide to strength
Healed the hole that ripped in living

In my book of dreams
In my book of dreams
In my book of dreams

The spine is bound to last a life
Tough enough to take the pounding
Pages made of days of open hand

In my book of dreams
In my book of dreams
In my book of dreams

Number every page in silver
Underline in magic marker
Take the name of every prisoner
Yours is there my word of honor

I took your urgent whisper
Stole the arc of a white wing
Rode like foam on the river of pity
Healed the hole that ripped in living

In my book of dreams
In my book of dreams
In my book of dreams

angel

How does it feel to fly
on such a silver wing?
To feel the air bow before
your feathered curve, your hollow bone?

Did you once tell me your name
So I would never be among strangers?

And have you come to say
What every city pigeon knows?
It's better to be living than be dead.

THE SILVER LADY

(Age 15)

When I was a little girl
Younger than nine or ten
I once spoke to the Silver Lady
But I never saw her again.

To me she flew out of the sky
She was born riding on the water
Her hair blew all around her
She was the crazy man's only daughter.

I used to see her every day
Riding her golden pony
Only once did I hear her laugh
And it echoed far and lonely.

Once I watched the river run
And I wandered too far from home
There I met the Silver Lady
She was crying, all alone.

I said, "Lady, why are you crying?
If I had wings like you
I would be flying over this river
And singing like only birds do."

Well she threw back her head and she smiled at me
Her tears, how they shone in the sun
She said, "I have no wings to fly with
If I did I would surely be gone.

"My brothers have all gone far away
To follow their hearts and be free
But I am the youngest and my father is aging
And all he's got left is me.

"I love my father dearly
Madman though he may be
It would break his heart if I should leave him
But this life is killing me.

"I feel the ocean pulling me
The breezes come and tell me things
I want to go with them wherever they go
And see what the new morning brings."

So she sadly turned away from me
So I stumbled my way back home
The next day I heard she had taken her horse
And gone off to parts unknown.

Her father stayed inside his lonely house
And he never more came into town
He could be seen roaming the riverside
And they say that he jumped in and drowned.

Long though I waited, she never returned
But when I felt a silver breeze
I knew she had sent it from wherever she was
To tell us that now she was free.

WOODEN HORSE
(CASPAR HAUSER'S SONG)

I came out of the darkness
Holding one thing
A small white wooden horse
I'd been holding inside

And when I'm dead
If you could tell them this
That what was wood became alive
What was wood became alive

In the night the walls disappeared
In the day they returned
"I want to be a rider like my father"
Were the only words I could say

And when I'm dead
If you could tell them this
That what was wood became alive
What was wood became alive

Alive
And I fell under
A moving piece of sun
Freedom

I came out of the darkness
Holding one thing
I know I have a power
I am afraid I may be killed

But when I'm dead
If you could tell them this
That what was wood became alive
What was wood became alive
Alive

acknowledgments

Lyrics (in order of appearance)
Solitude Standing © 1987 WB Music Corp. (ASCAP) / Waifersongs Ltd. (ASCAP)
As a Child © 1992 WB Music Corp. (ASCAP) / Waifersongs Ltd. (ASCAP)
Neighborhood Girls © 1985 Waifersongs Ltd. (ASCAP) / WB Music Corp. (ASCAP)
Daniella © 1976 by Suzanne Vega
Ironbound/Fancy Poultry © 1987 WB Music Corp. (ASCAP) / Waifersongs Ltd. (ASCAP)
Tom's Diner © 1987 WB Music Corp. (ASCAP) / Waifersongs Ltd. (ASCAP)
The Boulevardiers © 1981 by Suzanne Vega
The Rent Song © 1981 by Suzanne Vega
Straight Lines © 1985 Waifersongs Ltd. (ASCAP) / WB Music Corp. (ASCAP)
The Marching Dream © 1980 by Suzanne Vega
The Queen and the Soldier © 1985 Waifersongs Ltd. (ASCAP) / WB Music Corp. (ASCAP)
Knight Moves © 1985 Waifersongs Ltd. (ASCAP) / WB Music Corp. (ASCAP)
Luka © 1987 WB Music Corp. (ASCAP) / Waifersongs Ltd. (ASCAP)
Not Me © 1981 by Suzanne Vega
Bad Wisdom © 1992 WB Music Corp. (ASCAP) / Waifersongs Ltd. (ASCAP)
Lolita © 1996 WB Music Corp. (ASCAP) / Waifersongs Ltd. (ASCAP), all rights administered by
    WB Music Corp. (ASCAP) / Wyoming Flesh Publishing (ASCAP)
Those Whole Girls (Run in Grace) © 1990 WB Music Corp. (ASCAP) / Waifersongs Ltd. (ASCAP)
Feather and Bone © 1981 by Suzanne Vega
Rock in this Pocket © 1992 WB Music Corp. (ASCAP) / Waifersongs Ltd. (ASCAP)
In the Eye © 1987 WB Music Corp. (ASCAP) / Waifersongs Ltd. (ASCAP)
When Heroes Go Down © 1992 WB Music Corp. (ASCAP) / Waifersongs Ltd. (ASCAP)
Men in a War © 1990 WB Music Corp. (ASCAP) / Waifersongs Ltd. (ASCAP)
Institution Green © 1990 WB Music Corp. (ASCAP) / Waifersongs Ltd. (ASCAP) / Redrubber Music
    (ASCAP)
Private Goes Public © 1992 WB Music Corp. (ASCAP) / Waifersongs Ltd. (ASCAP), all rights
    administered by WB Music Corp. (ASCAP)
Woman on the Tier (I'll See You Through) © 1996 WB Music Corp. (ASCAP) / Waifersongs Ltd.
    (ASCAP), all rights administered by WB Music Corp. (ASCAP)
Big Space © 1990 WB Music Corp. (ASCAP) / Waifersongs Ltd. (ASCAP) / Redrubber Music (ASCAP)
Song of Sand © 1992 WB Music Corp. (ASCAP) / Waifersongs Ltd. (ASCAP)
Fat Man and Dancing Girl © 1992 WB Music Corp. (ASCAP) / Waifersongs Ltd. (ASCAP) /
    Wyoming Flesh Publishing (ASCAP)
One World (for *One World One Voice*) © 1990 Virgin Records Ltd. / One World Week Ltd.
Tired of Sleeping © 1990 WB Music Corp. (ASCAP) / Waifersongs Ltd. (ASCAP)
Calypso © 1987 WB Music Corp. (ASCAP) / Waifersongs Ltd. (ASCAP)
In Liverpool © 1992 WB Music Corp. (ASCAP) / Waifersongs Ltd. (ASCAP)
First Day Out © 1975 by Suzanne Vega
Men Will Be Men © 1992 WB Music Corp. (ASCAP) / Waifersongs Ltd. (ASCAP), all rights
    administered by WB Music Corp. (ASCAP)
As Girls Go © 1992 WB Music Corp. (ASCAP) / Waifersongs Ltd. (ASCAP)
Stockings © 1996 WB Music Corp. (ASCAP) / Waifersongs Ltd. (ASCAP), all rights administered by
    WB Music Corp. (ASCAP)
Marlene on the Wall © 1985 Waifersongs Ltd. (ASCAP) / WB Music Corp. (ASCAP)
Headshots © 1996 WB Music Corp. (ASCAP) / Waifersongs Ltd. (ASCAP), all rights administered
    by WB Music Corp. (ASCAP) / Wyoming Flesh Publishing (ASCAP)
(If You Were) In My Movie © 1992 WB Music Corp. (ASCAP) / Waifersongs Ltd. (ASCAP)
Casual Match © 1996 WB Music Corp. (ASCAP) / Waifersongs Ltd. (ASCAP), all rights
    administered by WB Music Corp. (ASCAP) / Wyoming Flesh Publishing (ASCAP)
Lightning © 1986 WB Music Corp. (ASCAP) / Waifersongs Ltd. (ASCAP), all rights administered by
    WB Music Corp. (ASCAP) / Famous Music Corp. (ASCAP)
Freeze Tag © 1985 Waifersongs Ltd. (ASCAP) / WB Music Corp. (ASCAP)

Photos / Sketches by (in order of appearance)

(title page)	Marion Ettlinger
(As a Child)	Suzanne Vega
(Fat Man and Dancing Girl)	Melodie McDaniel
(Leonard Cohen Interview)	Melodie McDaniel
(Leonard Cohen Interview)	Melodie McDaniel
(Watertown)	Michael Batal
(As Girls Go)	Ruven Afanador
(On Being Photographed)	Suzanne Vega (self-portrait)

about the author

SUZANNE VEGA is an award-winning songwriter and recording/performing artist who has performed on many of the world's great stages, including New York's Carnegie Hall and Radio City Music Hall, and London's Royal Albert Hall. Her recordings have sold in excess of six million copies worldwide.